The Author

C. PETER WAGNER is presently a faculty member of the Fuller Theological Seminary School of World Missions and executive director of the Fuller Evangelical Foundation. He originally delivered the contents of this book as lectures at Fuller School of Missions during the 1970-71 winter quarter. His missionary experience includes sixteen years in Bolivia, under the Andes Evangelical Mission.

He has also written *Condor of the Jungle, Defeat of the Bird God, Latin American Theology, The Protestant Movement in Bolivia, An Extension Seminary Primer,* and *A Turned-on Church in an Uptight World.*

Frontiers in
Missionary Strategy

Frontiers in
Missionary Strategy

By
C. PETER WAGNER

MOODY PRESS
CHICAGO

© 1971 by
C. PETER WAGNER

Library of Congress Catalog Card Number: 72-181592

ISBN: 0-8024-2881-9

Except where indicated otherwise, all scripture quotations
are taken from The New Scofield Reference Bible (New
York: Oxford U., 1967), with italics added.

Printed in the United States of America

*To my missionary colleagues
of the
Andes Evangelical Mission
and the
South America Mission—
brothers, companions in labor, and fellowsoldiers.*

Contents

Introduction

C. PETER WAGNER is one of my former students, a graduate of Fuller Theological Seminary, where I used to teach in the field of missions. I knew him and his wife better than many other students because they lived next to my wife and me, and we enjoyed a more intimate relationship that has continued across the years.

I followed the Wagners' pilgrimage when they elected to serve Christ as missionaries in Latin America. I read their prayer letters with delight and watched the growth of their family, as well as Peter's development as a first-class missionary who later held an important administrative post in the Andes Evangelical Mission. It was no less satisfying to see him turn to the printed word, and to read the books that began to flow from his fertile mind and facile pen. I was especially delighted by his obvious fascination for missionary theory and practice. It was this interest that led to this book, one that I might well wish I had written myself but one that is beyond my present knowledge and capacity. Surely there is no higher encomium for a teacher than that which comes when one of his students outshines him in his own speciality.

There are aspects of this provocative book that some missionaries and mission executives won't like. They shouldn't, because Wagner pinpoints certain weaknesses of modern missionary endeavor. He makes it plain, for example, that a number of missionaries should never have gone overseas; and he has tough things to say about the missionary call and the missionary candidate. In a biblical and pragmatic fashion he argues that missionary endeavor should yield a harvest. If it doesn't, something is wrong and somebody is to blame. In effect, he says that unproductive missionary work means money and manpower have been squandered. And this ought not to be. Judged on this scale, a proportion of present missionary work is a waste of time and money. The conclusion should be clear: a business-like approach means that the acid test for missionaries is that they reproduce themselves or they ought to go home and let somebody else do the job.

Wagner, along with other concerns, takes a hard look at Kenneth Strachan's theorem about evangelism-in-depth. While he does not rule out the concept, he finds flaws that suggest the necessity for rethinking and revising the concept both from a theoretical and a practical viewpoint. I think his criticism is well taken and hope the proponents of evangelism-in-depth will consider seriously what he has to say and come up with revisions of the theorem or a defense of it.

Basically, Wagner's book calls for the development of a workable missionary strategy, a theme that has not received the attention it deserves among evangelicals. His zeal springs from an understanding of and commitment to McGavran's church growth principles. Wagner asserts that successful missionary work requires much more than mere physical presence. It takes into account the people, their culture, and their responsiveness to the gospel. It searches out the facts from which a successful strategy can be fashioned. It answers, in advance of missionizing, the *how* to successful evangelization and offers concrete suggestions for developing a self-propagating church that will pick up where foreign missionaries leave off.

I think this book should be read by every mission executive and missionary. But more than that, it should be read by ministers and laymen who then should ask whether their financial investment in missionary outreach is yielding an adequate return and if not, why not.

Wagner does not pretend to be infallible nor does he intimate that the last word has been written. Indeed, I hope that this is the first salvo of what should become a continuing quest to make missionary strategy the subject of serious scrutiny, leading to the development and refinement of tactics that will produce maximum results.

HAROLD LINDSELL
Editor
Christianity Today

Preface

IF IT IS TRUE that we are in the "sunrise of missions," clear thinking on missionary strategy is an essential priority for the contemporary Christian church. This book is an attempt to set some guidelines for the development of a strategy which, while being evangelical and biblically-oriented, is also pragmatic and effective.

Special appreciation is expressed to those students of the Fuller Theological Seminary School of World Mission who, during the winter quarters of 1970 and 1971, participated in the forging of these ideas in the classroom. This book is an outgrowth of those highly tentative and unpolished lectures. It is still considered a tentative presentation of missionary strategy, but hopefully more polished.

In a sense, this volume is the farewell note to my sixteen years of residence in Bolivia as a missionary. It has been written as a result of many lessons learned from missionary colleagues, Bolivian evangelicals, and association with others who have thought through these problems much more profoundly than the present author. I would like to pay special tribute to the three who perhaps have influenced my thinking the most: the late Dr. Edward John Carnell, who as professor of theology opened my mind to theological creativity unfettered by classical systems of dogmatics; the Reverend Joseph S. McCullough, distinguished General Director of the Andes Evangelical Mission, under whom liberty and guidance were freely given to experiment with some of the ideas herein expressed; and Dr. Donald A. McGavran, whose impact upon the author while a graduate student in 1967-68 caused a radical reconstruction of his entire outlook on missions and missiology.

Finally, I would like to acknowledge my gratitude to Doris, my wife, who provided encouragement and consolation while these lectures were being given and this book being written, who cheerfully endured the long absences from home while I was teaching, and who then persisted under trying circumstances to complete the typing of the final manuscript. In her, "patience hath had its perfect work" (Ja 1:4).

Acknowledgments

GRATEFUL ACKNOWLEDGMENT is given to the following publishers and authors for permission to reprint copyrighted material from the titles listed below:

Creation House, Carol Stream, Illinois, for permission to quote from *Memo for the Underground* by Ted Ward, © 1971.

Fleming H. Revell Company, Old Tappan, New Jersey, for permission to quote from *The Master Plan of Evangelism* by Robert E. Coleman, © 1964.

Harper & Row, Publishers, New York, for permission to quote from *Who Shall Ascend* by Elizabeth Elliot, © 1968; and *The Social Conscience of the Evangelical* by Sherwood E. Wirt, © 1968.

John Knox Press, Richmond, Virginia, for permission to quote from *Christian Reality and Appearance* by John A. Mackay, © 1969.

Los Angeles Times, Los Angeles, California, for permission to quote from the article, "Off the Field, Players Do Not Mix So Well," copyright, 1968, *Los Angeles Times*, by Charles Maher. Reprinted by permission.

Lutterworth Press, Woking, Surrey, England, for permission to quote from *The Unfinished Task* by Bishop Stephen Neill, © 1967.

Moody Press, Chicago, Illinois, for permission to quote from *Revolution in Evangelism* by W. Dayton Roberts, © 1967.

Prentice-Hall, Inc., Englewood Cliffs, New Jersey, for permission to quote from *Missionary, Go Home* by James Scherer, © 1964.

The Reader's Digest, for permission to quote from the article, "Those Fabulous Italian Designers" by James Michener in the September 1969 *Reader's Digest*.

Time, Inc., New York, N.Y., for permission to quote from the article, "The Faith of Soul and Slavery," reprinted by permission from *TIME, the Weekly Newsmagazine;* Copyright Time Inc., 1968, From the April 16, 1968 issue.

13

1

Why a Missionary Strategy?

IN CONTEMPORARY MISSIONARY CIRCLES a curious suspicion of strategy permeates the thinking of many, from home churches to missionary executives to the grass-roots field worker. According to much current thinking, we might need to plan strategy in other fields of human activity, but missionaries are simply sent out to the field to "do missionary work." Jesus has promised to be with them "even to the end of the age." He will see that they accomplish their purposes, and results will come by the Holy Spirit.

Ultimately, it is true: the Holy Spirit is the controlling factor in missionary work, and the glory for results goes to Him. But, for reasons we have not been informed of, God has chosen to use human beings to accomplish His evangelistic purposes in the world. These human beings, missionaries in this particular case, may well become obstacles to the work of the Holy Spirit, just as they may well be effective instruments in God's hands. Some missionaries, unfortunately, have been victims of carnal motives, laziness, shallow knowledge of the Word of God, self-centeredness, unwise procedures, and lack of flexibility. As a result, their work has been fruitless.

Missionary strategy is never intended to be a substitute for the Holy Spirit. Proper strategy is Spirit-inspired and Spirit-governed. Rather than competing with the Holy Spirit, strategy is to be used by the Holy Spirit. It is used to empty the vessel of the missionary enterprise precisely so the Spirit can accomplish what He wishes to do in the world. Good management and careful planning have a definite part in all phases of the work of the kingdom of God, not excluding missions. To set them over against the Holy Spirit is improper, and detrimental to the Lord's work.

WHAT IS STRATEGY?

Strategy is a mutually-agreed means to achieve the ends which have been determined by a particular group. Good strategy will be concerned with broad principles as well as specific tactics, but it will not lose sight of the determined goal. The need for some strategy or other is evident in all fields from brain surgery to basketball. It is unnecessary only when no goals have been set, when those involved do not know precisely where they are going or perhaps do not care.

Such ignorance or indifference should never be a part of missionary work. Servants of God must have clear goals and know how to articulate them. Through prayer, the study of the Scriptures, and mature common sense they should have also a clear idea of how they are expected to reach the goals. Missionary strategy should, therefore, be characterized by these three essential qualities: Bible-centeredness, efficiency, and relevancy.

Bible-centeredness. Secular fields are not concerned that their strategy be biblical. Missionaries are, however, since the Lord's work must be done the Lord's way. It is true that sincere Christians might not fully agree in their interpretation of certain passages of the Bible and therefore come to differing conclusions as to what the Lord's way really is. But the Bible is reasonably clear as to the ultimate purposes of God, and one of the objectives of the material in this book will be to make as careful investigation as possible of the mind of the Lord in missionary work. The Bible, naturally, will be the principal source.

Efficiency. Missionary resources are limited, and presumably they always will be. For this reason the Bible has much to say about stewardship, or the responsible use of resources available. Efficiency is just another term for good stewardship.

In missionary work, stewardship over material resources is important. But the spiritual state of men and women without Christ adds a dimension which produces eschatological urgency. If improper use of resources might mean that some would spend a Christless eternity, Bible-believing Christians are rightly concerned about efficiency.

Efficiency includes, first of all, the best use of personnel. Many missionaries are not employed in the most effective service today, and as a result some aspects of God's work are retarded. Some of our appeals for more missionaries should be counterbalanced by more efficient use of the missionaries now on the field. Secondly, the best use of financial resources is called for. Since every mission budget I know of is limited, it is evident that decisions have to be made as to where money is spent and where it is not. This involves strategy, since priorities must be set. Finally, the best use of time must be considered for efficiency. Most missionaries are busy people. They work long hours. But questions must be asked as to whether the busyness is in fact helping reach the goals established.

Relevancy. Missionary strategy can go out of date very rapidly. Strategy for the 1970s in many aspects will be quite different from that of the 1960s. Even from one year to another, adjustments must be made in strategy to keep abreast of changing times. This is not always easy and, if consistently applied, makes missionary work more complex than it would be if no conscious strategy were involved at all. Keeping up to date requires diligence, wide reading, flexibility, consultation, planning, and a measure of courage. But it pays dividends.

WHAT ARE OUR GOALS?

According to our definition of strategy, goals are an essential prerequisite. If there are no goals, no strategy can be developed. Therefore, a thorough understanding of missionary goals is the first step toward the formulation of an effective strategy.

Goal-setting is a risk. One of the most comfortable things in the world is to have no goals, because then there can be no failures. It is equally comfortable to define your goals in terms of what you happen to be doing at any given time. If you shoot first, then draw the target around the bullet hole, you'll never miss the bull's-eye. If someone looks later, he might even call you a good marksman. Some people considered good missionaries by their friends have developed this technique well. Their goals are set more by their own inclinations than by carefully-formulated biblical priorities.

What are the biblical priorities? The vertical dimension involves faithfulness to God, while the horizontal dimension involves compassion for men. Let's look at them one at a time.

FAITHFULNESS TO GOD

First Corinthians 4:1-2 says, "it is required in stewards that a man be found faithful." Unfortunately, this verse at times has been misapplied to justify unproductive missionary work. Some have said, "If I'm just faithful to God, He will not expect results from me. He will produce the results Himself." The parable of the talents (Mt 25:14-30) shows that this is not always the case. A faithful steward is expected to produce results from the resources he has at his disposal. Proper use of resources is, in the parable, the difference between a "good and faithful servant" and a "wicked and slothful servant." As the parable suggests, the Lord establishes the goals, provides the resources, and then holds missionaries responsible to reach them.

One particularly unsuccessful missionary said to me, "It's true that I may not have accomplished much outwardly, but it has helped me draw closer to the Lord. After all, our relationship to God is what really counts in missionary work!" This statement contains enough truth that any contradiction of it could sound terribly unspiritual. It is subjective enough to be comfortable, because closeness to God is a quality extremely difficult to measure. But is closeness to the Lord a valid criterion upon which to evaluate a missionary's work?

God calls certain Christians to be missionaries for purposes slightly different from making them better Christians. Worship, prayer, a pious life, and a close walk with Christ are equally as important for a Christian plumber or librarian or advertising executive as they are for a missionary. Success or failure in the specific task are measured by other standards, according to the specified goals. A Christian surgeon, for example, should diligently cultivate his relationship to God. But, if his patients continually die on the operating table, he rightly will be considered a poor surgeon, although he may be a fine Christian.

By the same token, a missionary may be an admirable Christian person; but, if he fails to reach his goals, it should not be considered out of order to recognize the fact that he is a poor missionary. One of the problems in modern missions is that this is rarely done.

If successful missionaries are those who faithfully recognize the goals that God has set, and use the resources available to reach these goals, the next logical question is What are these goals specifically? In the context of the triune God, these goals can be discerned in relationship to each person of the Trinity: Father, Son, and Holy Spirit.

THE WILL OF THE FATHER AS REVEALED IN THE OLD TESTAMENT

Since the Bible is a unity, one would expect to find God's goals for missionary work revealed in the Old Testament as well as in the New. Granted, the clarity of some of the New Testament teaching is not to be found in the Old Testament; but nevertheless, the outlines are there. The people of God in the Old Testament were the Jews. God had set some goals for the Jews in relationship to the other nations, who were not included among the people of God.

"That men may know that thou, whose name alone is the LORD, art the Most High over all the earth" (Ps 83:18). Jehovah, the God who created the universe and God of the Jews, desired that all mankind come to know Him. This line of God's will for the salvation of the nations stretches from Genesis through the prophets.

In the books of the law, God's love for those who do not yet know Him is clearly expressed in the covenant with Abraham: "In thee shall all the families of the earth be blessed" (Gen 12:3). In the historical books, the confrontation of Elijah, the prophet of Jehovah, and the prophets of Baal is described in detail. The result of this power encounter was the recognition on the part of the spectators that "The LORD, he is God" (1 Ki 18:39). The spectators were the backslidden people of Israel, but other passages make it clear that God desires that same confession to spread to others. The psalmist says that God looked down from heaven "to hear the groaning of the prisoner; to loose those that are appointed to death, to declare the name of the LORD in Zion . . . when the people are gathered together, and the kingdoms, to serve the LORD" (Ps 102:20-22). The goal? "So the nations shall fear the name of the LORD, and all the kings of the earth thy glory" (v. 15). God's will for the salvation of mankind, then, comes through in the law, history, and poetical books. It is also expressed by the prophets.

One of the clearest Old Testament revelations of God's will for the nations is found in Isaiah 45. The nations are in a tragic situation because "they have no knowledge that set up the wood of their carved image, and pray unto a god that cannot save" (v. 20). The message that will bring them from the darkness to light is "Look unto me, and be saved, all the ends of the earth; for I am God, and there is none else" (v. 22). Again God's goals are spelled out: He desires "that unto me every knee shall bow, every tongue shall swear" (v. 23). Israel, the people of God in the Old Testament, like the church of the New Testament, was responsible to bring the nations to a knowledge of the true God, Jehovah.

THE LORDSHIP OF THE SON IN THE NEW TESTAMENT

He who claims Christ as Lord is committed to unquestioning obedience to His commandments. The first task of a faithful servant is to reach an accurate understanding of his Lord's will; and his second task is to accomplish it, regardless of the cost. Unfortunately, not all Christians are willing to do this. Such Christians should realize that they have little right to use the term *Lord*, when they refer to Christ.

The main purpose of the incarnation was summarized by our Lord when He said, "For the Son of man is come to seek and to save that which was lost" (Lk 19:10). He purposes to find the lost and provide salvation for them. In order to accomplish this, in His grace, He has elected to use His people, Christian men and women. Before He left the earth, Jesus made sure His followers had clear instructions as to what His will was for them.

The New Testament contains many commandments for Christians to obey; but, in relationship to our theme of missionary strategy, one of these commandments stands far out above the others. It has been given the title "Great Commission" and is found among the very last words that our Lord left with His disciples before ascending to heaven. It may well be that the very chronological position of the Great Commission in the teaching of Christ was designed to impress upon all generations of Christians its vital and supreme importance.

Those who take the lordship of Christ seriously, recognize how vitally important it is to understand the Great Commission; for without a thorough understanding of it, no one could be sure he was obeying it properly. The first step in understanding it is to recognize that it contains two major emphases, one concerning the means and the other the end.

The means toward accomplishing the end are witness and preaching. This is recorded by Mark, Luke, and John. Mark says, "Go ye into all the world and *preach the gospel* to every creature. He that believeth and is baptized shall be saved; but he that believeth not shall be damned" (16:15-16). Luke records this statement from Jesus: "Repentance and remission of sins should be *preached* in his name among all nations, beginning at Jerusalem" (24:47). Then in Acts, "Ye shall be *witnesses* unto me both in Jerusalem, and in all Judea, and in Samaria, and unto the uttermost part of the earth" (1:8). John adds, "As my Father hath sent me, even so send I you" (20:21).

Since these statements of the Great Commission stress the means, they should not be used in isolation from those which stress the end. Unfortunately, this is a rather common practice in some missionary circles; and as a result a truncated picture of the true thrust of the Great Commission is projected. Missionary strategy based on an inadequate understanding of this key New Testament concept will necessarily be faulty. It must be remembered that the Great Commission is witness and preaching, but it is more than that.

The end or goal of the Lord's commission to His people is described most clearly in Matthew 28:19-20: "Go therefore and *make disciples* of all the nations, baptizing them in the name of the Father and the Son and the Holy Spirit, teaching them to observe all that I commanded you" (NASB, italics added).

Of the four action verbs in this statement of the Great Commission, three are participles while only one is imperative. The imperative, *matheteusate* (make disciples) is clearly the goal of the Great Commission. The participles describe three means which will aid in accomplishing that goal: *poreuthentes* (going), *baptizontes* (baptizing), and *didaskontes* (teaching). Like preaching and witnessing (which Matthew also mentions in 24:14 and 26:13), these activities are essential parts of God's program but never ends in themselves. They all should be used as a part of the process of making disciples. Preaching is a *pre*soteric (before salvation) activity, baptizing is a *con*soteric (with salvation) activity, and teaching is a *post*soteric (after salvation) activity. All are involved in the cyclic process of making disciples.

If making disciples is the true will of God for missionary or evangelistic work, the term *disciple* must be defined precisely. The thinking of some missionary strategists at this point is often very imprecise. Some popular definitions err by being too broad, and others by being too narrow.

The overly-broad definition of *disciple* includes all those who might raise their hands in an evangelistic campaign, sign decision cards, or graduate from a confirmation class and take their first communion. None of these are accurate descriptions of *disciple,* any more than considering as disciples all those born and reared in a Christian country or those baptized as infants in their church.

On the other extreme, two common definitions make the term *disciple* narrower than the New Testament does. The first is to equate *disciples* with the twelve. If taken alone, Matthew 10:1-2 could give the impression that they are synonomous; but the parallel passage in Luke 6:13 explains that He called His disciples and "of them he chose twelve, whom also he named apostles." Of approximately 260 uses of *matheteus* (disciple) in the New Testament (these uses, incidentally, are all found in the gospels and Acts), only about twenty-five refer to the "twelve disciples." The rest have the much broader connotation.

A more frequent overly narrow definition of *disciple* makes him a person who has reached a somewhat advanced form of the Christian life. Particularly in those evangelical Bible conferences where the "victorious life" is stressed, this definition is often assumed. According to this point of view, not all Christians are necessarily disciples. Becoming a disciple is set forth as a challenge to Christians who attain a certain degree of victory or sanctification.

An artificial distinction between evangelism and making disciples has been made by some who would state: "Evangelism is just getting people saved, but this does not fulfill the Great Commission which says, 'make disciples.' This means bringing the believers into the stature of the fullness of Christ." This statement seems to imply that young, newborn Christians are not yet disciples; only those who have the "fullness of Christ" qualify.

In a widely circulated and excellent book on evangelism, Robert Coleman speaks of "converts" and "disciples" in a way which could lead the reader to think that Coleman is defining *disciple* in a manner we consider overly narrow. He says,

> The great commission is not merely to go to the ends of the earth preaching the Gospel (Mk. 16:15), nor to baptize a lot of converts into the Name of the Triune God, not to teach them the precepts of Christ, but to "make disciples"—to build men like themselves who were so constrained by the commission of Christ that they not only followed, but led others to follow His way [1964:108-109].

Perhaps this reflects a confusion of the teacher-disciple relationship of Paul and Timothy, for example, with the more technical use of *disciple* in the New Testament. Top biblical scholars are in agreement that *mathetes* does not describe a particularly advanced stage of Christian maturity but rather a basic relationship to Christ. Pierson Parker says, " 'Disciple' is the most frequent and general term for believers in Christ" (1962:S.V.). J. D. Douglas says, "The most common use of *mathetes* was in denoting the adherents of Jesus . . . believers, those who confess Jesus as the Christ" (1962:312). Kittel's *Theological Dictionary* adds, "The usage is from the very first characterized by the fact that, apart from a few exceptions, *mathetes* denotes the men who have attached themselves to Jesus as their Master" (1967:IV:44).

Faulty exegesis has been the cause of some confusion concerning this narrow definition of disciple. Passages such as Luke 14 set forth certain conditions for discipleship, such as leaving father and mother, denying one's own life, bearing his cross, and forsaking all he has (vv. 26-27, 33). It must be recognized, however, that these words were spoken to the multitude of interested people who were considering *becoming* disciples (v. 25). Jesus was attempting to "check this light-hearted manner of following Him" (Geldenhuys 1950:397). He wanted to be sure that *potential* disciples "understand that following Him involves a great deal" (Plummer 1901:363). In no way was our Lord here implying that some Christians were not disciples.

An even more difficult passage is found in John 8. Since most of our translations begin verse 31 with "Then said Jesus to those Jews who believed on him" it sounds as if the next clause, "If ye continue in my word, then are ye my disciples indeed" is spoken to Christians who possibly have not reached discipleship. This is not the proper interpretation, however. The New English Bible correctly identifies the people Jesus was talking to as "the Jews who had believed him," contrasting it with the last part of verse 30, "many put their faith *in* him." B. F. Westcott brings out the exegetical implications of this when he says,

> They *believed Him* and did not *believe in Him*. The addition of the word "Jews" and the change in the construction of the verb distinguish sharply the group (of v. 31) from the general company in v. 30; and the exact form of the original makes the contrast more obvious [1951:133. Italics added].

The men whom Jesus was talking to may have been convinced of His Messiahship, but they interpreted His teachings according to their own prejudices. That's why Jesus later said of them, "Ye are of your father the devil" (v. 44).

As implied in Acts 11:26 and with few exceptions, disciples and Christians are synonomous. A disciple is a person who has been born again by the Spirit of God. He has confessed with his mouth the Lord Jesus and believed in his heart that God has raised Him from the dead (Ro 10:9). He is a new creature in Christ Jesus. He may have his ups and downs. Peter was a disciple even in those dark days when he denied his Lord three times, trembling at the thought of the cross. Joseph of Arimathaea was "a disciple of Jesus, but secretly for fear of the Jews" (Jn 19:38). But in general the life of a disciple is characterized by continuing "steadfastly in the apostles' doctrine and fellowship, and in breaking of bread, and in prayers" (Ac 2:42). In Antioch the disciples were called Christians, and we will find today that the most helpful definition will make the same equation.

The Great Commission commands Christians everywhere to make "disciples" or (born-again) Christians, of "all nations." This clearly implies that it is God's will that multitudes of men and women become true disciples of His son.

One of the opponents of church growth is a bit hasty when he says, "What neither McGavran nor any of his disciples (including Wagner) has proved is that the New Testament gives a basis for equating the 'make disciples' of the Great Commission with the 'multiply the number of converts to Christianity' implicit in the church growth theory" (Padilla 1971: 101). If "converts" means those who are regenerated in the full theological sense of the word, this is exactly what the Great Commission *does* command the servants of the Lord to do. It is nothing less than the order of the King.

THE MINISTRY OF THE HOLY SPIRIT IN THE WORLD

A thorough understanding of God's revealed goals for evangelistic or missionary work as a basis for strategy will take into account not only the revelation of the will of the Father in the Old Testament and the lordship of Christ in the New but also the ministry of the Holy Spirit in the world.

In general terms, the four principal dimensions to the work of the Holy Spirit in evangelistic work include conviction, proclamation, regeneration, and perfection. God's Spirit, as the paraclete, *convicts* the world of sin, righteousness, and judgment (Jn 16:8). He convinces men that they have sinned and come short of the glory of God. Through *proclamation*

He purposes to inform every man that "God so loved the world, that he gave his only begotten Son, that whosoever believeth in him should not perish, but have everlasting life" (Jn 3:16). Christ is proclaimed as the liberator. The Lord wills that none "should perish, but that all should come to repentence" (2 Pe 3:9). When a person repents of his sin, the Holy Spirit works a miracle of *regeneration* in his life (Titus 3:5). making him a new creature in Christ Jesus (2 Co 5:17). Following that, the Holy Spirit begins a lifelong process of *perfection* in the life of each disciple, guiding him into all truth (Jn 16:13).

If these are the four dimensions of the evangelistic work of the Holy Spirit, how do they apply to planning strategy for men and women who desire to serve Him? The answer to this important question begins with the recognition that only one of the four is accomplished by the direct action of the Spirit, that of regeneration. The other three are accomplished not directly but through the ministry of properly prepared human beings. Because regeneration, the creation of a new nature within the human person, is an infathomable miracle, no human cooperation at all is called for. Even in the other dimensions of His evangelistic ministry, it must be recognized that the Spirit does not *need* human help. To need assistance is an absurd possibility for omnipotence. But in His divine wisdom, the Spirit has *decreed* a measure of human responsibility; and it is left for us to accept this fact, not to question it.

In order to prepare the members of the body of Christ for a responsible part in evangelistic work, the Holy Spirit performs three special ministries. First, He gives the appropriate and necessary gifts to each member of the body. No Christian is left without a gift, and all are expected to use their gifts to the utmost for the glory of God (1 Co 12). Secondly, God fills His servants with power, all the power needed to accomplish the goals He has set for them. Christ advised his first disciples, "tarry ye in the city of Jerusalem, until ye be endued with power from on high" (Lk 24:49). Finally, the Spirit sends out gifted and Spirit-filled Christians to make more disciples. At the church of Antioch He said, "Separate me Barnabas and Saul for the work unto which I have called them" (Ac 13:2).

Through the ages, the Holy Spirit has repeated this process over and over to accomplish His purposes in the world. He prepares men and women and expects them to cooperate with Him in the supreme task of world evangelism. Well-planned and Spirit-governed missionary strategy helps God's servants to be the best possible instruments in His hands.

Compassion for Men

If the vertical dimension for understanding God's goals in missionary work is faithfulness to God, the horizontal dimension is compassion for men. The Bible stresses both.

The two greatest commandments of God are "Thou shalt love the Lord, thy God, with all thy heart, and with all thy soul, and with all thy mind. This is the first and great commandment. And the second is like it, Thou shalt love thy neighbor as thyself" (Mt 22:37-39). All the law and the prophets are summarized in these two commandments. Obedience to either of them leads to the imperative of effective evangelism. Love of God implies faithfulness and obedience. As we have seen, this compels a Christian to go and make disciples of all nations. But love of man leads to similar action.

Love of man includes simultaneous concern for his physical, material, and social needs as well as his spiritual needs. True Christian compassion does not erect false dichotomies which separate body and soul. But realistic Christian concern will recognize the awesome importance of the final destiny of each person. If I love my neighbor, I will want to see him fed, clothed, cured, and well adjusted. I will want to see also that he is not going to hell, doomed to an eternity separated from God. In this attitude I am sure to be in agreement with God, since God does not desire that even one of his creatures perish.

This means that I must communicate the gospel to my neighbor, pray for him, and under the guidance of the Holy Spirit, persuade him to become a Christian. Compassion will lead us to sincere evangelism. This is the horizontal dimension of biblical priorities.

If these are valid principles, missionary strategy based on them will beware of seeking without finding or sowing without reaping. Making disciples must be maintained as the central objective of missions, without allowing good-sounding phrases to detour efforts toward secondary goals. In a recent appeal for funds to support a radio broadcast, the promoter said, "What we know is that one of these broadcasts reaches more people than the number of people a missionary couple would be able to reach personally in a year of time."

This is a misleading statement since it establishes the vague and secondary goal of "reaching" people as the basis for appraising the relative value of a radio broadcast as over a missionary couple. The crucial question, avoided by this imprecise promotional terminology, is not how many people may or may not be "reached" but how many disciples are made as a result of a particular ministry. One suspects that in this case the radio ministry may be an example of seed-sowing evangelism.

Not only will strategy based on biblical priorities seek the ultimate goal of making disciples, but it will also attempt to make the maximum *number* of disciples possible. The total effectiveness of evangelistic work then may be evaluated in these terms. This involves the use of numbers, a practice frowned upon in some missionary circles but used to good advantage in others. Missionary Paul Enyart tells a rather humorous story of one official missionary report which reflected an unusual nervousness about numbers. After hazarding a guess that the number of believers was about 2500, the report commented: "It is not always best to number Israel." A page or two later, the same report continued: "On the mission farm there are 201 chickens, 17 mules, 2 burros, and 8 steers, heifers and calves" (1970:43).

GETTING THE BLOOD OFF YOUR HEAD

Faithfulness to the will of the triune God and loving compassion for men are the two principal biblical motives for making disciples. Care should be taken, therefore, that evangelistic motives do not become egocentric. A subtle form of this may be seen when one proclaims the gospel in order that he "discharge his responsibility," or "be delivered of the blood of the person who hears," as Ezekiel 33:1-11 suggests. An overly rigid application of this passage to evangelistic work can result in a very hurried, superficial, and unfruitful effort. Proclamation can become impersonal to the point of a failure to communicate. In its extreme, it focuses more on the benefits to the preacher ("thou hast delivered thy soul") than on those who need to enter the kingdom of God.

This is not to say that, if Christians fail in their evangelistic responsibility, they will not be held accountable. They will, just as a watchman who does not sound the proper warning will be held guilty of the blood of those who suffer the consequences. But as a *motive* for evangelistic work, getting the blood off one's head is a short circuit. It has led to making bigger and better trumpets with gimmickry and gadgetry and "gospel blimps," with little concern as to how many people in fact obey the message. It has blurred the true motive of evangelistic work, the "make disciples" of the Great Commission.

HINDRANCES TO MISSIONARY STRATEGY

The curious aversion to the business of strategy planning which already has been mentioned needs some analysis at this point. To one degree or another, all of us involved in missionary work have been guilty of hindering the development of good, sound missionary strategy. Some of the causes of this can be pinpointed; some are more subtile. Here are five of the more obvious ones:

1. WE HAVE BEEN TOO STRONGLY TIED TO TRADITION AND CULTURE

Several recent writers have been pointing out how closely associated with the status quo our present church structures tend to be. Some churches and some missions seem to have built-in inertia. Many of us are all too content to continue our missionary program the way it always has been done. It seems that an excessive amount of energy would be needed to re-evaluate the past and take the creative steps necessary to reach the goals of making disciples in the future. Knowing this is a very difficult and often threatening procedure, few have been willing to spend the time and effort needed to clarify strategy.

James Michener recently wrote a fascinating story for *Reader's Digest* about the Italian designers. It ought to be a model for missionary strategists. A group of about forty clever, hard-working artists are remaking Italy itself as well as setting standards of design for many other parts of the world. Top manufacturers such as Olivetti and Necchi order their designers to "restudy the whole problem of the machine, then determine how it ought to look in a modern world, ignoring all previous concepts" (1969:158-59). If missionary leaders could bring themselves to apply the same techniques to their enterprises, the direction of modern missions would be significantly altered.

Change, of course, is not intrinsically good. Nothing should be changed just for the sake of change. But on the other hand, the temptation to resist change should be conquered. Openness to changes, large and small, will keep a mission program from becoming irrelevant and passé in our rapidly changing world. While fear of change is common, obedience to Christ is a far stronger motivation, and this often requires a degree of insecurity and risk. Abraham accepted risk when he left Ur of the Chaldees.

All innovation and change require a certain willingness to experiment. The basis of any experiment is a hypothesis, an idea of how to do something better. The experiment is designed to test the new idea. Built into the process is the understanding that the idea might prove to be a good one or a bad one. An unsuccessful experiment should not be considered a failure but rather a valuable block of knowledge which will help to construct something more successful in the future. Some timid folk are unwilling to experiment because they dread the possibility of failure. If this were a universal attitude, the world would still be in the Stone Age. Unfortunately, some of our missionary programs seem to be taking on some Stone Age characteristics for this very reason.

2. WE HAVE NOT BEEN TRAINED TO DIAGNOSE THE HEALTH OF
   A CHURCH

As we think back to our missionary training programs in Bible institute or seminary, it becomes evident that many of them were not fully geared to prepare the students for effective missionary work. Surprisingly few missionaries have learned precisely how to go about the task of diagnosing the health of a sick church and prescribing the proper remedy to restore health.

One of the indications of this is the widespread indifference to statistics exhibited by missionaries. As anyone who has attempted to write an analytical study of growth of the churches in a given area knows, accurate and meaningful statistics are extremely difficult to come by. Without statistics it is very difficult to diagnose the health of a church. It is like a physician attempting to diagnose a sickness without being able to use a thermometer. Much of our missionary work is still in the witch doctor stage of development, when it should be emerging into the era of aseptic surgery.

3. WE HAVE BASED STRATEGY DECISIONS ON "NEED."

"We must move missionaries into West Zax. They have such a tremendous need there." This type of statement has been repeated over and over again as sufficient justification for assignment of missionary personnel. But when examined in the light of strategy and goals, it has little meaning. Since all people without Christ have equal need, it becomes a self-neutralizing term when applied to missionary work. Granted, people without Christ have more need than Christians; but if we return to the imperative of the Great Commission—that of making disciples—we are talking only about strategy for doing this among non-Christians, all of whom need Christ equally.

"Need" therefore is not a good starting point for developing strategy, since it doesn't help in making any separation between those needy non-Christians who are recepitve to the gospel and those who are not. Both groups have the same need, but both are not of equal priority in missionary strategy. If personnel and other resources are available to move into a disciple-making ministry on only one field, how can a choice be made between possibilities A, B, and C?

Some might suggest the number of churches already planted. It might appear that if A and B already have churches, C would be the field of most need, and therefore we would move there. But often the presence of churches, especially growing churches, is one of the most accurate signs of potential fruitfulness at a particular time, and the lack of churches an indication that a people have rejected the gospel and will staunchly refuse to become disciples. The place with the most churches might not seem to be that with greatest need under current standards, but it might be the place of top strategic importance as far as effective evangelisitc work is concerned.

Likewise, a study of the comparative rates of growth of the churches in A and B might be wrongly used if "need" were the criterion. If the churches in B are growing much more slowly than in A, the conclusion might be that B has more need. But it could also be true that an investment of mission resources in B would produce scant results over a five-year period, while an equal investment in A would reap an abundant harvest. Criteria other than apparent need must be used.

Some have postulated the greatest "need" on where there are fewest missionaries in relationship to national believers. This is not necessarily a valid point, as we will see in the next chapter. The law of the harvest demands that laborers, whether missionaries or nationals, be sent to the harvest field in the greatest number possible, as long as each is reaping to his capacity.

The deceptive use of "need" is to base strategy on how many previous evangelistic trips have been made to a certain region. This is the fallacy of "no-one-should-hear-twice-until-everyone-has-heard-once." Such an evangelistic philosophy is based on a reversal of primary and secondary goals. The secondary goal often described as "reaching people" or "proclaiming the gospel" is made the primary goal of evangelism rather than the true Great Commission imperative of making disciples. It produces superficial evangelistic work in many cases and should be avoided.

"Need" at times confuses the issue in other areas of missionary thinking. The question has been asked, Is there a need for missionaries on our field now that we have a strong national church? This question is misleading, since a strong national church does not necessarily reduce the need for missionaries. Here is a better way to phrase the question: Are there men and women on our field who can be won to Christ by Spirit-filled missionaries? If the answer to this one is yes, then there is a true need as well as an opportunity for missionaries; and other things being equal, there is no reason to think that it might not be God's will for missionaries to continue.

4. WE HAVE USED THE HOLY SPIRIT AS A SMOKESCREEN

Although this is a delicate topic, it should be pointed out that in some cases the Holy Spirit has been utilized as a very subtle smokescreen to hide from view other, more valid reasons for fruitless missionary effort. These subterfuges are worded so that expecting a seed-sowing effort to produce a harvest seems to be rather unspiritual. In an article on the subject, Does the Great Commission require great success? the implied answer was that God sometimes expects little fruit. The author gave an example of workers who went to preach to a certain people and reaped no results; then she asked, "Why do they fail?" The answer was that perhaps our premise is at fault in naively making goals for God that He never intends to reach. This suggested solution was substantiated by the fact that God has left us with many mysteries—mysteries which no plan can comprehend, no magnanimous effort can challenge, and no strategy can solve.

A closer analysis of this point of view (mentioned here only because it is so typical of this mentality) reveals errors both in theory and practice. In theory, it makes the mistake we warned against previously, of using only half of the Great Commission as the biblical basis of evangelistic work. After quoting the Great Commission as "Go into all the world and preach the gospel to the whole creation," it asks, "Will our success not be judged in terms of obedience to God, whether those to whom we preach hear, as was Paul's experience, or do not hear, as was Isaiah's?" The fact of the matter is that Jesus left a very clear command as to His will when he said to *matheteusate,* make disciples. Making disciples is no naive human objective but rather the clearly revealed will of God.

On the practical side, one of the major problems of the workers in question was that they did not learn the language of the people they were trying to evangelize. Preaching is a most important means toward the end of making disciples, but only preaching that communicates. Preaching must allow the people not only to hear the gospel in their own language but consider it in their own cultural context so that the gospel is relevant to them and becoming a Christian is a valid option for them. This was not the case in the article mentioned and may well have been the answer to the "mystery" of failure.

Verses like "God . . . giveth the increase" (1 Co 3:7) and "no man can come to me except the Father, who hath sent me, draw him" (Jn 6:44) do not negate the expression of the will of God in the full-orbed Great Commission. Rather they stress that, in spite of the fact that the Holy Spirit uses human instruments to accomplish His evangelistic purposes in the world, the final product—new disciples—is entirely His work. No human glory is involved. Mission is God's work.

Another author, whose excellent literary gifts almost cloud the real issue says, "We must resist the glamorous temptations of statistics, persist for the long, hard pull. Diamonds take longer to grow than toadstools." This may lead us to believe that meager fruit for evangelistic efforts has a diamondlike quality, while an abundant harvest is most likely to be nothing but toadstools. This is what is meant by putting up a smoke-screen.

5. WE HAVE SUBSTITUTED GOOD ACTIVITIES FOR MAKING
   DISCIPLES

Someone has rightly said, "The good is the eternal enemy of the best." Really, hardly anything a missionary does is "bad." We all are doing a good work in one sense or another. Mission public relations organs, including prayer letters, often have been geared toward convincing supporters to approve whatever we are doing, rather than providing the type of information that would enable them to make an independent judgment as to what returns they might be getting on their investments. Since much of this camouflages the true goals, supporters are deprived of the measuring sticks most needed against which to match performance.

One missionary reporter, describing a work he had observed, said "This kind of evangelism is a fantastic work for the Lord and produces a rich harvest of souls." Most of us have tended to report our work in this kind of imprecise terminology, so this is not pointing the finger at some isolated case. We have given the impression that for the public to require more precise reporting of missionary work is carnal. Suppose someone reading this report wrote to the missionary involved and asked for an accounting of his stated goals in terms of the population of the area, the percentage of these people that are hearing the gospel, the response in terms of disciples made, the number of churches planted, rates of growth in existing churches, etc.? The missionary involved would in all probability accuse this person of meddling and consider him out of order for asking such questions.

In this area, the lack of a clearly articulated missionary strategy has set Christian missions apart from nearly every other field of activity. It seems that it is time this situation be corrected. Why missionary strategy? Because with it we all will be more effective instruments in the hands of the Lord of the harvest.

2

Biblical Principles for a Strategy of Missions

ADEQUATE MISSIONARY STRATEGY must be based on correct biblical principles. As has been mentioned already, the Lord's work must be done in the Lord's way. Many churchmen agree that, of several recent attempts at defining the biblical basis of mission made by contemporary missiologists, the definition by Professor Donald McGavran of Fuller Theological Seminary is among the most relevant and preceptive. The publication of *The Bridges of God* in 1955, to some, marked the inauguration of an entire new era in the history of modern missiology. The subsequent establishment of the School of World Mission and Institute of Church Growth at Fuller Seminary, which now has gathered a faculty of six, has served to reinforce this opinion.

Not that McGavran and his colleagues have been without criticism. Some harsh opposition has come chiefly from two sectors. First, the radical theologians see McGavran's insistence that God wills multitudes of people to become Christians and multitudes of churches to be planted and to grow in every receptive group of people on earth, as a threat to the promotion of revolutionary social justice, particularly when the institutional church is seen as an instrument of preservation of the status quo. Secondly, some evangelicals who are involved in good evangelistic and missionary activities but for one reason or another have been relatively static and fruitless, see McGavran as a threat because he so staunchly appeals to objective analysis in terms of measurable goals. In emotionally-laden attempts to discredit the whole school of thought, some have even charged McGavran and his colleagues with "ecclesiolatry," "numerolatry," or some other form of idol worship.

36

In spite of this criticism, some of which has been constructive and has helped in producing certain modifications of church growth theory, this book acknowledges its debt to McGavran and his colleagues for their fresh insights into biblical truth. It is not necessary that one declare himself a disciple of McGavran in order to be a good mission strategist. But at least full consideration should be given to new insights into certain teachings of the Word of God as a basis for understanding God's will in contemporary missionary work.

THE CHURCH GROWTH THEORY AS THEOLOGY

Some of the criticism of the church growth school of thought, even by friends, has been that it lacks theological content. This charge merits a close examination, for it has been the cause of some misunderstanding.

There is no doubt that church growth principles are highly theological. That they give the impression they are not is partially due to an overly technical definition of theology. In its most basic sense, *theology* signifies any statement which is made about the nature of God Himself or the relationship of God to His creation. The simple phrase "God is" must be recognized as a theological statement. Even a fleeting examination of the writings which have come out of the School of World Mission at Fuller Seminary will convince the reader that theology is being written there. The repeated statements about God, the church of Christ, God's will, biblical commandments, the Holy Spirit, revelation, the people of God, and so on—all have profound theological content and connotations.

Why, then, do critics like Donald Flatt of the Lutheran School of Theology in Chicago make statements such as:

> The church growth school has not taken seriously enough the responsibility of developing an adequate theological basis. It therefore loses the support of many able missiologists, who otherwise might accept its goals and insights [1970:20].

There are undoubtedly many reasons why church growth has projected a negative theological image as far as some observers are concerned. Five which occur at the moment are as follows:

1. Church growth is a very specialized field of theology. It concentrates on only one subpoint of the traditional theological encyclopedia, that of ecclesiology. Within ecclesiology, it narrows down even more to the field of missiology. The theological implications of most of the other divisions of systematic theology have been taken for granted up to now rather than dealt with explicitly in church growth theology. There is no doubt that the particular missiology now being developed by the School of World Mission needs to be related more and more to other theological disciplines in the future.

2. A new vocabulary has been developed which sounds rather exotic and nontheological to many who hear it for the first time. It is easy to see how one who had not been previously introduced to such phrases as *Africasia, seed-sowing evangelism, multiindividual conversions, organic growth, extension seminary, modules and sodules, redemption and lift, perfecting disciples, remnant theology, horizontal church structures, persuasion evangelism,* and scores of others coined by church growth men, would feel slightly "out of it." Especially those looking for a theology stated in traditional phraseology would be disappointed at the first reading of church growth material. Little wonder they would react negatively—not only to the unfamiliar terms but, as a result, also to the principles they express—and counter by saying, "This is *not* theology!"

3. This negative reaction on the part of some who *do* take the effort to master terminology is expressed in other terms which excuse them from any further consideration of the matter. They attempt to write off church growth teaching as unworthy of any scholarly consideration by accusing it of lacking theological content. It would be more honest for these men to state their position not in terms of "church growth has no theology," but rather "I disagree with church growth theology." There is no question that the boldness with which McGavran and his colleagues attack ineffective theory and practice of missions has produced emotional reactions. But, as the Old Testament eloquently indicates, no prophet of any age can expect much different treatment.

4. Church growth theology is difficult for some to accept because it ordinarily requires an active response. The theoret-

ical aspect is so intimately related to the practical that, unlike other theological pursuits, mere contemplation will not suffice as a response.

In the field of technology, a pattern of action called "Mooer's Law" describes some limitations in the human sphere to the almost boundless information that is becoming available through the employment of computers. It goes like this:

> The use of an information system is dependent on the amount of new effort required by the recipient to act on the information. The more effort it will require, the less likely it is that the information system will be used [Dayton 1971:1].

Some reactions to church growth theology reflect Mooer's law. Since an adequate response to it would involve a great deal of effort to absorb, evaluate, and act upon the content of this rapidly growing body of literature, some say "What's the use?"

5. While it should be admitted that church growth theology exists, it also should be admitted that it has not yet been wrapped in a recognizable theological package. In the first chapter was mentioned a group of Italian designers, some of whose qualities missiologists would do well to imitate. But some of the designers did too good a job. One of the best, Achille Castiglioni, said,

> In 1956 I designed one of the best things I ever did—this vacuum cleaner. Instant success! Major art journals in all parts of the world carried stories about it. Industrial magazines hailed it. The Museum of Modern Art in New York exhibited it in a study collection. Prizes everywhere. But one fault. When the salesmen saw it, they cried, "It doesn't *look* like a vacuum cleaner." The machine was manufactured in small quantities, but practically no one bought it. The design was too advanced. One of my best things, and it landed in a museum! [Quoted in Michner 1969:159].

Like consumers, contemporary Christians have been conditioned to look for a certain package. Theology, in order to be properly dealt with, must follow a certain outline, use certain technical terminology, interact with the ideas of certain contemporary elites, and deal with certain historical issues. If it is not wrapped in this package, it will not be considered theology by many Christians, no matter how much it might talk about God.

Since church growth men are invariably missionaries who have had experience in cross-cultural communication, they undoubtedly will be among the first to acknowledge that church growth theology must be properly wrapped. Just as church growth writings must be translated into Japanese or Arabic in order to communicate them properly, the theory itself must be translated into "theologese." No one has yet done this because few missionaries are made in the image of the stereotyped theologian. Perhaps in the near future someone with proper theological credentials will undertake the task of expressing church growth in theologese.

PRINCIPLES FROM THE PARABLES

The basic theological principles for church growth emerge from exegetical studies of the history of salvation, the relationship of the people of God with the heathen nations in the Old Testament, the purposes of Christ's incarnation and the application of redemption as expressed in the Great Commission, New Testament teachings on the relationship of the church to the world, the imperative of Christian obedience to the lordship of Jesus Christ, the person and work of the Holy Spirit, and other major biblical and theological topics. Some of this theological groundwork was discussed in the previous chapter, but it is not the purpose of this book to deal with the theological as much as the practical aspects of Christian missions.

While theology is revealed through such doctrinal passages, strategy is revealed through more practical portions of the Bible. As He trained His disciples, Christ often used parables to drive home important principles for their later ministry. It is for this reason that we turn to the parables in an attempt to understand some of the broader strokes of missionary strategy taught in the New Testament.

One of the shortcomings of contemporary Christianity is to look at the parables as quaint preindustrial stories and therefore interpret them quite superficially. Christ used a great deal of agricultural terminology to communicate with His disciples because they were products of a rural culture. Although it may require an effort, those among us who are urban-oriented should attempt to understand the parables as farmers would. If we succeed in assuming a farmer outlook, we can learn much concerning Christ's counsel for missionary strategy.

THE BASIC AGRICULTURAL PRINCIPLE

Basic to the mentality of a farmer is the vision of the fruit. This is expressed in broad terms in John 4:35-36:

> Say not ye, There are yet four months, and then cometh harvest? Behold, I say unto you, lift up your eyes, and look on the fields; for they are white already to harvest. And he that reapeth receiveth wages, and gathereth fruit unto life eternal, that both he that soweth and he that reapeth may rejoice together.

Sowing and reaping are both important, but both are only means to an end. Why does a farmer sow and cultivate and reap? Only to get the fruit, for his very livelihood depends on producing fruit.

In missionary work, some have lost the vision of the fruit. Some have fixed their attention on novel methods of sowing the seed, with at best a vague hope that someone, sometime, might harvest something. This may well be a major cause of the ineffectiveness of much missionary work in the world today. Sowing is essential, but no farmer is satisfied with sowing only. Jesus premised His parables on this vision of the fruit, which did not need previous explanation to His disciples. They understood.

BASIC AGRICULTURAL LAWS

Three basic agricultural laws can be discerned in the teachings of Jesus: the law of sowing, the law of pruning, and the law of harvest. Let us examine them in more detail.

1. *The law of sowing.* The parable of Matthew 13:1-23 has been called "the parable of the sower," following Jesus' own lead in verse 18. This title, however, can be misleading if it is allowed to prejudice the interpretation. A preferable title for the purposes of interpretation would be "the parable of the soils."

Why is this?

Of the four divisions of the parable (the roadside, stony soil, a thorny field, and good soil), three for one reason or another fail in the basic agricultural objective of producing fruit. One succeeds. A farmer would immediately ask, "What is the factor that made the difference?"

Several things are constant through the parable. The sower is the same man, who presumably uses the same method. The seed is the Word of God and does not vary. No mention is made of the climate, which we may assume is constant. Only one variable is present: the soil. The obvious lesson for a farmer is that even the best seed will produce the desired fruit only if it is sown in fertile soil. No amount of effort, hope, desire, or prayer can make seed sown on the roadside bear fruit. Sowing the seed is necessary, but this parable refines the concept and teaches that *intelligent* sowing is necessary if the proper harvest is to come as a result.

The obvious principle for missionary strategy is that, before sowing the seed of the Word, we will do well to test the soil. Not all peoples of the world, of a given country, of a certain ethnic group, or even of a city are equally fertile soil for producing fruit thirty-, sixty-, and a hundredfold. God has prepared some but not others to receive the Word of God and bow their knee to the lordship of Jesus Christ. Today God is providing tools that missionaries of a generation ago did not have for distinguishing between the fertile soil and the barren soil. As much as possible, responsible missionary strategists should strive to eliminate careless or broadcast sowing, since not only does this fail to produce fruit but it also feeds the devil ("the fowls of the air devoured it"; "then cometh the devil, and taketh away the word out of their hearts" [Lk 8:5, 12]).

Interestingly enough, while the New Testament commands Christians to sow and to reap, there is no parallel command to plow or prepare the soil. Arguments from silence prove little, but at least this omission raises a question in our minds: Might not this task of preparing the soil be an area which God has reserved for His own sovereign actions in the world? Perhaps He does not wish human cooperation in this aspect of the work.

If this is so, we would do well to rethink many of our programs of what has been called preevangelism.

Some have said that it doesn't matter what kind of soil the seed lands on, for God has said, "My word . . . shall not return unto me void" (Is 55:11). The context of Isaiah's prophecy, however, deals with the mystery of the way God's common grace works with mankind as a whole, not with the specific evangelistic responsibility of the New Testament church. Furthermore, a reading of the history of missions as well as the personal experience of many missionaries indicates that God's Word *has* been proclaimed many times without bearing fruit because it has landed on barren soil. The parable of the soils clearly warns against this very thing.

2. *The law of pruning.* The parable of the barren fig tree in Luke 13:6-9 describes the law of pruning. There we have a tree which is planted, grows, seemingly flourishes, but bears no fruit. A conflict arises between the hired man who cares for the plant, and the owner. The hired man, fascinated by the tree in which he has invested so much of his tender, loving care, seemingly has formed somewhat of an emotional attachment to it. The owner, however, is not so much interested in the beauty of the fig tree, as in figs. He has kept in clear focus the vision of the fruit.

Much missionary work, unfortunately, is like the fig tree. There is much to see, and much to take pictures of. The work has "grown." But even after decades of arduous labor, it has borne little or no fruit.

The farmer of the parable feels that three years is adequate time for this fig tree to produce fruit. However, he accedes to the pleas of the hired man to give it one more year ("just let me stay here until furlough") but then insists that, if no fruit is forthcoming, the resources (in this case, the ground it occupies) should be used for something that will in fact produce fruit.

Missionaries would do well to apply this principle of trial and error to all their work. If the objective from the beginning is to reap fruit, emotional ties with the work which will blur this vision should be avoided. The mobility necessary to leave unfruitful works after an adequate trial period and move on to fruitful works would do a great deal to increase the evangelistic effectiveness of many missions. Naturally, there is nothing sacred about three or four years as a trial period: and therefore every worker needs to seek God's guidance as to the timing. But whether the period is long or short, the law of pruning should not be forgotten.

3. *The law of the harvest.* This law is expressed by Jesus in the phrase, "The harvest truly is plenteous, but the laborers are few. Pray ye, therefore, the Lord of the harvest, that he will send forth laborers into his harvest" (Mt 9:37-38).

For the first time in the succession of agricultural principles, the need for an increased number of laborers is mentioned. Any farmer will confirm that harvest time is the most critical as far as workers is concerned. Sowing and pruning allow more tolerance than harvesting. If the right quantity of harvesters is not available at the right time, much fruit may be lost. If this happens, all the good sowing and pruning will have been in vain.

Not all fields ripen at once. Good farm management, as well as good missionary strategy, will place the bulk of the workers in the ripest field but not abandon the others, since someone should be on hand to do the work when the harvest is ripe there, too. The most common missionary error is to deploy an excessive number of workers in fields where the harvest is not yet ripe; while at the same time in the ripened harvest fields, fruit is being lost because of lack of workers. Jesus' prayer request for laborers in the *whitened* harvest fields is the law of the harvest.

JESUS' EXAMPLE

Right after speaking of the whitened harvest in Matthew 9, our Lord set an example for the application of the principle in Matthew 10. This portion relates how He called the twelve and sent them out to preach the message that "the kingdom of heaven is at hand" (Mt 10:7).

Jesus did not send out His disciples to broadcast the seed willy-nilly. Three basic ethnic groups inhabited the region: Jews, Gentiles, and Samaritans. Of the three groups, the Gentiles and the Samaritans were not receptive at that particular time, so Jesus said, "Go not into the way of the Gentiles, and into any city of the Samaritans enter not." Rather, they were to take the message to "the lost sheep of the house of Israel" (Mt 10:5-6).

Even among the Israelites, all were not equally receptive. The disciples were not to use their time on those who "shall not receive you, nor hear your words" (v. 14), in the same way that the hired man was not to waste his efforts on the barren fig tree. Anticipating this resistance, Jesus continued, "when ye depart out of that house or city, shake off the dust of your feet." This was sound missionary strategy for Jesus' day, and it is equally sound advice for us today. If more missionary mentality were geared to it, missions in general might now be much nearer to fulfilling the Great Commission.

PAUL'S EXAMPLE

Acts 17-18 gives us an example of how the apostle Paul applied these agricultural principles in his missionary work in Macedonia and Achaea. He was on his second term, by then an experienced missionary. In spite of that, he made some false moves, such as trying to go into Asia and Bithynia; so the Holy Spirit had to close the doors there and turn him away. Finally, in order to get him on the right track, the Holy Spirit had to give him the special Macedonian vision, which led him to Philippi.

During his previous term of service in Asia Minor, Paul had learned that God was opening up to him many doors to winning Gentiles to Christ. He also learned by experience in places like Salamis (Ac 13:5), Antioch of Pisidia (Ac 13:14), and Iconium (Ac 14:1), that one of the best bridges for reaching the Gentiles with the gospel at that time was the synagogue community. Each synagogue community of those days was composed of a mixture of hard-core Jews, proselytes, and God-fearers. The Jews were born into the synagogue community, but the proselytes and God-fearers were Gentiles who had voluntarily attached themselves. The proselytes had taken the rather decisive step of circumcision and full obedience to the law, while the God-fearers enjoyed many of the benefits of the

Jewish faith without desiring to submit themselves to circumcision.

In Philippi there was no synagogue. Instead Paul sought out the functional equivalent, the place "where prayer was accustomed to be made" (Ac 16:13), and won Lydia, one of the God-fearers, to Christ. This group was a particularly fertile field for the gospel in those days.

Six fields are mentioned between Philippi and Ephesus. Two of them, Amphipolis and Apollonia (Ac 17:1), were green, probably because they did not have synagogue communities. One, Athens, was slightly ripe. Only a minimal amount of fruit was forthcoming, such as Dionysius the Areopagite and Damaris (v. 34). But three were truly whitened harvest fields: Thessalonica ("of the devout Greeks a *great multitude,* and of the chief women *not a few,*" v. 4), Berea (*"many* of them believed; also of honorable women who were Greeks, and of men *not a few,*" v. 12), and Corinth (*"many* of the Corinthians, hearing, believed, and were baptized," 18:8).

Paul spent as much time as possible in the whitened harvest fields. He may well have stayed longer in Thessalonica and Berea if political pressures exerted by the resistant hard-core Jews had not been so great. The Jews tried the same thing in Corinth, but they were unsuccessful; so Paul stayed a year and a half.

We should note that places like Amphipolis and Apollonia had as much *need* for Christ as did Thessalonica and Berea. But Paul did not fall into the error of letting need determine his strategy, so he passed right through these needy places. He did not spend time there, because he knew he should get on to the true harvest fields where he could reap fruit thirty-, sixty-, and one-hundredfold. This is just a reminder not to let strategy be determined by need.

Was Paul's missionary strategy premeditated? The famous missiologist, Roland Allen, made a special effort to deny that Paul operated on a premeditated strategy. Allen said,

> I cannot help concluding then from this brief review that St. Paul did not deliberately plan his missionary tours. . . .
> . . . St. Paul plainly did not select where he would preach on grounds like these: he was led of the Spirit [1962:12, 16].

Certainly the Holy Spirit steered Paul and had to make him change course from time to time, as we have already mentioned. But generally speaking, it seems that Paul had accurately located the fertile fields ahead of time and that he expected a harvest there when he sowed the seed of the Word. Allen goes too far when he asserts that Paul "did not start out with any definite design to establish his churches in this place or that" (1962:17).

Looking to the Holy Spirit for definite guidance as to missionary strategy before one begins a missionary journey is no different in kind from looking to Him for guidance as to homiletical strategy before going into the pulpit. Definite plans for missionary work should not be considered unspiritual. Missionaries and mission executives need not be haphazard about planning their strategy, for the Spirit of God delights to give wisdom to those who prayerfully seek it. In no way is this a denial of the supreme fact that the mission of the church is the *Missio Dei,* the mission of God.

Generally speaking, the Holy Spirit will lead those who are willing to work into the harvest fields which are already white. At times, however, He may lead otherwise. Prophets such as Ezekiel and Isaiah were required to bring the message to a resistant people. Other prophets, such as Jonah, were sent to receptive peoples. We should regard the predetermined failure of Isaiah as an unusual leading of God, however. This is not the norm. Since God is not willing that any should perish, He delights in leading His servants out to peoples who have been prepared for the gospel and who will turn to Jesus Christ in abundance.

3

Keeping Mission Strategy Up-to-date

IN CHAPTER 1 we mentioned that effective missionary strategy must be kept relevant. One of the principal tasks of God's servants is to review and rethink what has been done in the past, and, like the Italian designers, come up with something which will meet adequately the new challenges that the world is forcing upon mankind. Because of our failure to do this, many of the methods which missions are using today are obsolete already. As George Peters says, "Culture is in convulsion and society in explosion. . . . Only dynamically functioning, well integrated and purposeful men will be able to function effectively in an ordered manner in such a world and achieve worthy goals" (1971:54).

Updating mission strategy is not always the most pleasant job, because many people do not welcome change. Content with the status quo, they feel threatened by something new which might force them to admit that "all has not been well in Zion." The Old Testament prophets were well aware of this attitude, which drove some, like Jeremiah, to tears.

Six broad areas can be discerned in which today's missionary strategy must be updated. To the degree it is, contemporary missions and missionaries may become more effective instruments in God's hands.

UPDATING HERMENEUTICS

Some missionary leaders continually stress the need to return to the first century. They have created a nostalgia so strong that in some circles all that is done today must be evaluated as to how nearly it approaches what was done nineteen hundred years ago. Two of the most distinguished missiologists of the twentieth century, Alexander Hay and Roland Allen, both show tendencies in their writings toward over-sanctifying the first century.

Hay, for example, says that he became disturbed when he discovered that "the methods we were employing in our work were not those used by the New Testament Evangelists or by our Lord, and that the pattern of our churches differed greatly from theirs" (1947:9). He admits that "it was no easy matter to discern what was really of the modern method and not in accord with the principles of the scriptural pattern"; but never-theless, he goes on to lament that "we may preach the same Gospel as the Apostles, but our methods of work are not the same methods they used" (1947:9, 18).

Hay is quoted here only as a representative of a rather large school of thought which stresses the first century too strongly. Some of the reasons for objecting to this mentality are given under the following subheads.

PRINCIPLES VERSUS METHODS

Good missionary strategy distinguishes clearly between prin-ciples and methods. On the contrary, Hay's tendency is to take the apostles' methods as principles. This is one reason he in-sists on one particular type of church government (the brethren assemblies pattern) rather than admitting that the church gov-ernment used by Paul and his colleagues was simply a wise and strategic use of certain first-century cultural patterns. These patterns were relevant to first-century Christians, but they may have little relevance to Christians who come from other cul-tures at other stages in history.

It is simply inaccurate to assume that churches structured along the lines that Hay recommends are receiving more of God's blessing or are growing faster than churches with dif-ferent structures. Hay, for example, rejects the idea of a min-ister or pastor who is paid a salary by the congregation for his role in leading the group. Nevertheless, the multiplying inde-pendent movements in Africa and the large Pentecostal churches in Chile seem to thrive under just this kind of govern-ment. It appears to be more culturally relevant to them than the structure that Hay would recommend.

PAUL'S HUMAN NATURE

When studying the apostle Paul as a missionary prototype, it helps to use the kind of emotional detachment that will allow us to evaluate his shortcomings as well as his successes. Paul was as human as any of us. He too was subject to error. While supernatural inspiration by the Holy Spirit protected him from error when he wrote his epistles, it does not follow that his missionary strategy was equally inspired or inerrant. If Paul had to remind the Lystrans that he was not a god, but a man "of like passions with you" (Ac 14:15), perhaps we also need that reminder.

Could Paul possibly have made a mistake in Athens, for example? Although he began with his normal strategy and went to the synagogue first (Ac 17:17), it seems that he might have permitted himself to become slightly overemotional about the pagan religions ("his spirit was stirred in him, when he saw the city wholly given to idolatry," v. 16); and perhaps he unwisely allowed the pagan philosophers to lure him onto their own ground. On Mars Hill, as he could have anticipated, he was sowing seed on barren soil, although his presentation of the gospel to those cultured and intellectual idolaters was absolutely brilliant. The harvest in Athens was minimal in comparison to some of the more responsive places he went to.

Happily, Paul was a big enough man to be sensitive to the leading of the Holy Spirit when he was wrong. Why did he turn up the road to Bithynia, for example? One can imagine that Paul and his companions held a field council meeting with a ten-page, single-spaced report on reasons for a trip to Bithynia before they even left. But the Holy Spirit intervened and told Paul that his well-laid plans were wrong. Paul then recognized his error and turned back, an experience that most of us have had at one time or another, largely because we are human. Paul was, too.

THE NEW TESTAMENT TODAY

When thinking through missionary strategy, it is much more helpful to attempt to fit New Testament principles into twentieth-century patterns than to attempt the reverse. In other words, we do well not to spend too much time lamenting over how bad we might be today, and how many of our present cultural characteristics need to be lopped off so we can look more like the first-century church. It is much more profitable to accept ourselves as we are now, and see how best to adapt New Testament principles to our present situation.

To help out in this process, someone ought to do a new paraphrase of the book of Acts, writing it in contemporary language. One could refer to Paul's terms rather than journeys. His time in Jerusalem and Antioch was furlough. The Jerusalem Council could have been a meeting of the mission board. Timothy could be called a junior missionary, and Mark a missionary intern. The Corinthians were a group of nationals. Paul's epistle to the Philippians was a prayer letter. If this were done, Acts would become a much more helpful book for contemporary strategy.

PAUL AS AN M_1 MISSIONARY

The apostle Paul should be recognized as what Ralph Winter would call an M_1 missionary. The fascinating classification of missionaries in the categories of M_1, M_2, and M_3 will be explained in the next chapter. But since Paul's ministry was not basically cross-cultural, as is the ministry of many contemporary missionaries, he is in the M_1 category. He did not have to learn a foreign language, go through the throes of culture shock, or even apply for a passport and visa. In some senses his situation was quite different from that of many missionaries today. This is another reason why it is improper to attempt to transfer Paul's missionary methods lock, stock, and barrel to the twentieth century.

UPDATING THEOLOGY OF MISSIONS

The current defeatist mentality has produced a defective theology of missions in many circles. Especially in the historical denominations, the kaleidoscopic theology that emerges seems to echo the gasps of a tired church. Pessimism and defeat are rationalized in theological terminology. When spiritual vitality is drained, theology turns to social issues and deemphasizes the imperative of the Great Commission; although the two should really complement each other. Since much theology reflects the jaded condition of the churches that produce it, it becomes to a degree ethnocentric. It speaks to conditions prevailing in churches of the sending countries, while conditions in the recipient churches are often vastly different. Little wonder that the theological debates of the Anglo-Saxon churches seem irrelevant to many Third World churchmen.

Tragically, evangelicals who could correctly discern the moving of the hand of God in the world today have not been developing the adequate theological alternatives to counteract the radical and humanistic theology emerging from the tired churches. Much theological work needs to be done in this decade by those committed to biblical priorities. Contemporary theology of mission needs to be updated in these following areas, among others.

DOCTRINE OF AUTHORITY

A low view of revelation and the inspiration of the Scriptures is characteristic of much modern missiology. Some writers lack clear conviction as to what the Bible teaches. Skepticism about the reality and power of demons is an example especially relevant to animistic people. In many recent writings, Scripture is introduced reluctantly, exegesis is weak, and hermeneutics are allegorical.

DOCTRINE OF MAN

In contrast to classic liberalism, man is now recognized as sinful. But man's sin is often described not so much as enmity with God on an individual basis as a collective offense to fellowmen on the social level.

DOCTRINE OF CHRIST AND CHRISTIANITY

Since Christianity is seen to be retreating, a post-Christian age is frequently postulated; and theology is brought into line with this assumption. Christ and Christianity are no longer seen as unique but as relative expressions of the work of God that can be seen also in other religions. Kaj Baago of the Union Theological College of Bangalore says,

> Must Buddhists, Hindus and Muslims become Christians in order to belong to Christ? . . . The answer is obviously "no." . . . Such a mission will not lead to the progress of Christianity or the organized Church, but it might lead to the creation of Hindu Christianity or Buddhist Christianity [1966:32].

Dominican Joseph Kenny, writing about Muslims, calls them people "who are in fact members of Christ" and even claims that in a sense they are members of the visible church (1970: 38).

DOCTRINE OF SALVATION

The new universalism has entered as the tired church's doctrine of salvation. It is no longer based on an overly optimistic view of man, as was the older universalism, but rather it is based on an overly generous view of grace. Redemption is seen in terms of social and cultural improvement. Donald Dawe says,

> The humanizing and renewal of religion in India (under the challenge of Christianity) to give rise to new forms of Hindu religion and social life may seem to us the hidden work of God. But is it not the redemptive work of God? [as quoted by Glasser 1971a:113].

DOCTRINE OF RECONCILIATION

Reconciliation is basically horizontal, man-to-man, man-to-society, or society-to-society, rather than vertical, God-to-man. Even in this horizontal dimension, reconciliation is seen as collective rather than individual.

DOCTRINE OF THE CHURCH

The church has outlived her usefulness. She should be crucified, dead, and buried. The institution must go. Therefore, making new disciples or losing old ones is not a primary theological concern. From the ashes, God will resurrect something new for the future.

DOCTRINE OF MISSIONS

The term *missions* has been changed to *mission*. This reflects a basic change in goals. Lesslie Newbigin explains it in these words:

> When we speak of "the mission of the Church" we mean everything that the Church is sent into the world to do—preaching the Gospel, healing the sick, caring for the poor, teaching the children, improving international and interracial relations, attacking injustice—all of this and more can rightly be included in the phrase "the Mission of the Church."
>
> But within this totality there is a narrower concern which we usually speak of as "missions." Let us, without being too refined, describe the narrower concern by saying: it is the concern that in the places where there are no Christians there should be Christians [1960:23].

Thus, the phrase *the church is mission* is more dangerous than it might first appear. It reflects a subtle but widespread shift in emphasis from making disciples as the top-priority missionary goal to simply doing good works in the world.

DOCTRINE OF EVANGELISM

Presence and social service have become the predominant forms of "evangelism" in much contemporary theology. Redeeming society is seen as a higher priority goal than individual salvation. This can be crippling to the missionary vision of the church. The Student Volunteer Movement, which was a powerful missionary force in the United States at the turn of the century, peaked in 1920 and then began a steady decline. Why? Partly because "their emphasis shifted away from Bible study, evangelism, lifework decision and foreign mission obligation on which the SVM had originally been built. Instead they now emphasized new issues such as race relations, economic injustice and imperialism" (Howard 1970a:92).

This thumbnail sketch of several of the crucial areas of modern theology of missions is designed simply to underline the critical need for updating. Viable and biblical evangelical alternatives must be presented with vigor and conviction if the proper theological base for mission strategy is to be laid for our generation. If this is not done, a widespread erosion of the missionary activity of the church is inevitable.

UPDATING ECUMENISM

The ecumenical movement was born from a missionary concern, articulated by the Edinburgh Conference of 1910. It was thought that visible unity of Christendom would be valuable "that the world may believe that thou hast sent me" (Jn 17:21). Through the years, however, priorities have been reversed until unity itself as a primary concern has replaced world evangelism. As one of the principal ecumenical architects, John Mackay now observes that

> unity is not for mission. Unity is for unity. This obsession
> with unity for its own sake, this movement toward oneness in
> sentiment and structure with no clear understanding of, or
> commitment to, the *task* of a united church locally or in the
> world, is what I call *ecumenicalism* [1969:86].

If unity can be used as a means toward helping the church fulfill the Great Commission, it is worthy of support and promotion. But in recent years, the great movements toward unity have not borne out the premise that unity in fact helps the growth of the church. Mackay says,

> My concern, however, is this: the dynamic missionary vision
> that created the "great new fact" is being replaced by an in-
> stitutional image which allures leading ecumenists. In conse-
> quence, the ecumenical movement tends to be less and less
> motion outwards and onwards toward the frontiers. It be-
> comes instead increasing motion towards the realization of
> an ordered, ecclesiastical structure. In a subtle manner dedi-
> cation to mission becomes merely the pursuit of harmony
> [1969:85-86].

The abandonment of original goals is one of the reasons for the growing dissatisfaction with the formal aspects of the ecumenical movement by those who see it from within. Lukas Vischer, for example, calls into question the relevance of the organization to the churches themselves. He says,

> It can be asked whether the World Council really is a fel-
> lowship of churches and not rather constantly in danger of
> being no more than an organizational superstructure floating
> above the Churches and not really supported by them [1969:
> 358].

Ecumenists, determined to escalate unity wherever possible, were successful in merging the International Missionary Council with the World Council of Churches in New Delhi in 1961. They argued that this would help, not hinder, the missionary movement in general. Not all agreed at the time, however. According to Peter Beyerhaus, "The opponents of the merger, particularly those tending toward the evangelical position, feared that mission would become inflexible and bureaucratic. Above all, they feared the likelihood of a change in its true spiritual goal" (1971:31). Unfortunately for the cause of missions worldwide, the worst has happened. Unity has been achieved at the expense of missions. As Beyerhaus wistfully comments *ex post facto,* "the great missionary awakening of the churches (which was expected from the 1961 merger of the International Missionary Council and the World Council of Churches) has not yet occurred" (1971:14).

A revealing editorial in *Christianity Today* recently showed how, during the three decades from 1938 to 1968, the missionary forces of the three major merged churches in the United States fell off, while that of nonmerged, but National Council of Churches related, churches rose slightly. Interestingly enough, the most dramatic rises in missionary forces occurred in the Baptist Church (which had split, rather than united, in those years) and in the churches and missionary societies not related to the NCC. The editorial concludes:

> The claim that church union advances the witness of the Church and enlarges its outreach lacks historical support, both as it relates to church growth on the home field and as it relates to missionary outreach abroad [1969:21].

The recent motto Unity in Witness and Witness in Unity, which is a part of the Roman Catholic-World Council of Churches study document entitled "Common Witness and Proselytism" (*Ecumenical Review* 1971:9ff), reflects an emphasis on inclusivism which can only tend to water down aggressive missionary programs of the churches. Concern for the feelings of fellow churchmen is in danger of overshadowing concern for full commitment of men and women to Jesus Christ. As missiology is accommodated to the central objective of unity, a gradual dilution of the theological imperatives of the Great Commission will result. Disturbed by signs of this regression in the fourth WCC Assembly in Uppsala, Arthur Glasser remarks that, "its concerns were neither ecclesiastical nor theological, but rather secular and horizontal—the world's agenda of social, political, and economic issues" (1969:144).

To the degree that ecumenical activity of any kind (including some efforts toward unity among nonconciliar evangelicals) deviates or detracts from the supreme mission of the church in the world, that of making disciples, immediate updating is called for.

UPDATING TECHNOLOGY

Technology is one of the facts of modern life. Any effort to relate the missionary strategy of the church to our contemporary world must take it into account. True, technology has many inherent shortcomings. These are being pointed out with vigor both by the younger generation in the developed countries and by spokesmen for the developing countries of the Third World. The concern that technology may tend to dehumanize man is a valid warning, and one that must be faced honestly and realistically by the church.

Among the pioneers in the use of technology in missions is the Missions Advanced Research and Communications Center (MARC) of World Vision International. The director of this center, Edward Dayton, has necessarily done a great deal of thinking about the validity of technology in Christian work. A correspondent once raised this question to him: "Are we not in danger of becoming so wrapped up in the power and efficiency of our tools that we become man-centered rather than God-dependent?" Dayton's answer is an excellent statement of the attitude which is most consistent with sound mission strategy:

> Yes. The risks are great. But the risks are equalled by the potential. We need to understand both. Most Christians with a real desire to proclaim Jesus Christ like to believe they would be willing to face the dangers of death or privation. . . .
>
> The dangers of failure are great. Will we neglect the potential because of the risks involved? God forbid! [1968:6].

In this section it would be impossible to exhaust the developments in technology which need to be applied by updated mission strategy to the opportunities in the world today. Some of
the more important, however, deserve to be discussed here.

TRANSPORTATION

Undoubtedly, aircraft will be used to a larger extent than
ever before in many fields. The need for missionary pilots will
increase. Perhaps many missionaries now on the field should
learn to fly, obtain their licenses, and become more mobile.
The transition from the automobile to light aircraft in countries where ground transportation is not yet well developed may
parallel the transition from the mule to the automobile of three
or four decades ago. At the same time, sound criteria as to
whether moving to aircraft will help or hinder church growth
must underlie each decision.

COMMUNICATIONS

Of the modern means of communication, radio and television have received a great deal of prominence. These media
can be powerful tools for evangelism. But at the same time,
they can easily become means of sowing without concern for
reaping. The fallacy enters when it is assumed that the evangelistic value of a given radio ministry, for example, is directly proportionate to the number of the potential listening
audience. McGavran, however, has shown how a radio broadcast in the Kui language beamed from Addis Ababa toward the
50,000 members of the Kuinga tribe might be strategically
more effective than a broadcast in Swahili which would have
a potential audience of the 60,000,000 Swahili speakers of
East Africa (1969:17). Little of this type of thinking has
been done in missionary communications, unfortunately.

Radio can be shown to have been effective as an instrument
of church planting. The Christian and Missionary Alliance
beamed their Spanish broadcast into Venezuela, where they did
not have a church. A questionnaire sent out brought a remarkable response of 519, which included 74 who had been
converted through the broadcast. Then a follow-up survey
team located groups of believers with no church affiliation who

wanted to start C&MA churches in Venezuela (*Alliance Witness* 1970:n.p.).

In 1962 the transmission by radio of a six-week evangelistic campaign in Guayaquil, Ecuador, was climaxed by a baptismal service in which 1500 were baptized before 30,000 spectators. The Foursquare Gospel, sponsors of the campaign, had one small meeting room in the city before the campaign but opened eight new churches afterwards (Weld 1968:62).

Many radio ministries need to be reexamined in light of biblical priorities of evangelism. Some radio work which was effective years ago now has become obsolete. Other radio and television evangelism is just coming into its own. But it should not be assumed that, simply because a program goes out over the air, it is fulfilling the ministry for which it was designed. One well-known evangelical radio broadcast, which was an effective tool for making disciples years ago, now continues as a Bible teaching ministry to Christians. As times changed, it was updated to keep pace with new conditions.

LITERATURE

The traditional mission-run, mission-oriented, and mission-subsidized literature program, which perhaps was useful for newborn churches in the Third World, is now being updated on many fields. One progressive mission now states that "our literature program is now a business with a ministry, rather than a ministry run somewhat like a business." Authors must receive royalties which will make their efforts worthwhile. Printers must be able to make a decent living from their trade, even if they specialize in Christian printing. Booksellers need a realistic markup. Customers must pay for what they get. Only in this way can a literature program become integrated into the economy of the particular country where it is operating, properly fitting into the context of the emerging church.

BEHAVIORAL AND SOCIAL SCIENCES

Modern developments in the behavioral and social sciences open up wide possibilities for missionary strategy, on which few mission leaders have been able to keep informed. The valuable insights that technicians in these fields can provide missions should be used in a much greater measure than they have been to date. This is why the delegates to the Elburn Consultation on Latin American Church Growth made the following recommendation:

> That consideration be given to recruitment of candidates trained in the social and behavioral sciences who will be qualified to act as consultants, giving direction to the most effective use of social and cultural dynamics for the growth of the church, missionary-national relationships, etc. [*Latin America Pulse* 1970:4].

SYSTEMS ENGINEERING AND COMPUTERS

Some of the procedures and techniques being designed and profitably used by industry today have direct applications to missionary strategy. New insights into efficient planning and management need to be employed for setting and evaluating missionary goals. It is not surprising that this appears threatening to some, but it should help greatly toward locating bottlenecks and correcting unproductive methods. McGavran describing the philosophy of the School of World Mission in Pasadena, says,

> We believe in pragmatically sound methods. We devise methods and policies in light of what God has blessed—and what He has obviously not blessed. Industry calls this "modifying operation in the light of feedback." . . . We teach men to be ruthless in regard to method. If it does not work to the glory of God, throw it away and get something which does [1970*a*: 3].

Stanley Mooneyham of World Vision is sensitive to the negative reaction to the image of the "huge, impersonal, whirring computer." Nevertheless he is outspoken in his encouragement of missionary leaders to make use of what technology has to offer today. "It will require vision and foresight, prophetic utterances, and projections that to many people will sound like sheer folly," he says. Then Mooneyham concludes that "the prophet in his time has always sounded foolish because he has been marching to a different drumbeat—the drumbeat of the passionate heart of his Lord" (1970:7).

UPDATING MISSIONARY PERSONNEL

In order to provide the personnel necessary for the implementation of missionary strategy, recruitment and deployment of personnel needs to be kept up-to-date. In the next chapter we will go into the details of spiritual gifts and missionary call, but here we simply will mention some of the newer emphases which should be included in overall planning.

With the worldwide educational explosion, some missions have been emphasizing higher and higher academic qualifications for missionaries. This is not always the best. As men like Paulo Freire and Ivan Illich are pointing out, the general educational standard of Third World countries in many cases is not rising, nor can it ever rise under present educational structures. A larger elite is receiving the benefits of modern education, but the masses in many countries such as Brazil are remaining at low educational levels. Although some missionaries with high academic achievements have the flexibility to minister effectively to those with little education, more likely missionaries who have similar educational backgrounds will be best able to communicate. If the masses continue to provide the most fertile soil for spreading the gospel, missionaries who can effectively minister to them must be recruited.

Theological educators in Latin America were surprised at the results of a recent survey conducted by the Latin American Committee on Theological Texts (CLATT) in an attempt to discover the relative academic levels of adult church leaders who had enrolled in the mushrooming programs of extension theological education. Of over three thousand who were tabulated, it was found that 72 percent had reached only the "certificate" (less than full primary education) level. This should be an indication to mission strategists who have the responsibility of recruiting personnel for the extension of the churches. That a college degree measurably helps communication with a semiliterate peasant is a questionable assumption.

This is not to say that missionaries on the higher academic levels are not needed. Especially in theological education and urban ministries, well-trained workers through the doctoral level are called for. But while we need to keep our recruiting on the high levels moving, we will make a mistake to *exclude* the lower-level candidates for academic reasons.

Increased emphasis on the gifts of the Spirit along with academic qualifications is required in missionary recruitment. The stress on this in some missions is a healthy sign, but in others no question about spiritual gifts is even asked on the candidate application papers. Personnel troubles are just around the corner when workers are assigned to responsibilities for which they have no spiritual gifts; and conversely, when workers who do recognize their spiritual gifts are not afforded adequate opportunities to use them. Emphasis on gifts brings emphasis on teamwork, which will help any program reach its goals. Missions which are a collection of individuals rather than a coordinated team cannot hope for much success.

Many missions now are starting what the Wycliffe Bible Translators have been doing for years: making use of support personnel. These are professionally trained people, such as pilots and radio technicians, who fill vital roles on the missionary team, even though they might lack the requirements that regular missionaries have to meet. The reasoning that a full course of training in seminary or Bible college is necessary for a missionary printer, for example, is fading. In some cases ministerial training has been detrimental to the performance of personnel for such positions as teachers in missionary children's schools. Many with ministerial training feel frustrated if they are not in a more directly church-related ministry, while those with full teacher qualifications but no Bible school degree feel well adjusted and useful in this important aspect of the Lord's work. Support personnel are usually happy to be freeing regular missionaries for their spiritual ministries.

Attitudes toward lifetime missionary service among young people have changed radically. Few in the present generation are willing to make unconditional lifetime commitments for the mission field. For this reason many are considering short-term service from a year or less to one full term. Some Christian laymen who enter early retirement offer themselves for service during their sunset years. Missionary intern programs and summer worker programs are opening up further opportunities for personnel which can be used in one aspect of missionary work or another. Dynamic missionary strategy will build all these new and variable factors into planning and management.

UPDATING PSYCHOLOGICAL CONDITIONING

A person's mental attitude toward his job has a powerful bearing on how that job is accomplished. This is as true of missions as it is of medicine; of evangelism as much as ecology. One of the great needs today is that of new healthy psychological attitudes which will help bolster the morale of missions and improve missionary strategy from the inside out.

Somehow we have allowed a dark cloud of pessimism to descend upon large sectors of the church in our Anglo-Saxon, missionary-sending countries. This needs to be dispersed so the brightness of the light of life can shine through once again. True, there is ample reason for pessimism in the Anglo-Saxon countries. Here are some brief notes from recent periodicals:

United States. Church attendance in the United States has dropped 7 percent since 1958, according to a recent release by the Gallup Poll.

United States. The United Methodist Church, second largest denomination in the United States, fell 201,096 in the past year, a drop of about 2 percent.

United States. The 1971 budget of the Board of World Missions of the Presbyterian Church US will require cutting the missionary force from 467 to 353.

Canada. Metropolitan Toronto population has increased by 50,000 annually, but United Church membership is declining by 3,000 per year.

England. A drastic cut—perhaps as much as one-third—of the Church of England's twenty-one seminaries is expected to follow a vote by the Church Assembly recognizing the problems created by a drop in ministerial candidates from 737 in 1963 to 431 in 1968.

Australia. The Presbyterian Church of Australia plans to have only forty-six missionaries at overseas posts in 1970. This is nearly 25 percent fewer than three years ago.

Some of this kind of news has led *U.S. News and World Report* to print in bold type: "At home, too, the missionary is under fire—from churchmen who say his day is finished" (1968:74). They quote the Reverend Ronan Hoffman of the Catholic University as saying,

> The era of foreign missionary movement is definitely over because the goals and objectives of that movement are no longer valid. . . . There has been a widespread assumption that the Church was destined to convert the entire human race to Christianity. This must be rejected as a valid goal because it has no biblical foundation. . . . I suggest that the Church voluntarily dismantle our present missionary organization and structure [1968:74].

Arthur Glasser detects some of the same pessimism in recent writings of Donald Dawe of Union Theological Seminary, Richmond. With a note of sadness, Glasser reports,

> With no attempt at documentation Dawe affirms that the outcome of missions, as with America's foreign aid program, has been "frustration and failure." As for the Church in Asia, Africa and Latin America, he dolefully concludes that "future prospects are not promising" [1971a:112].

For one thing, this type of mentality is not biblical. One wonders when Ronan Hoffman last might have read his New Testament. George Peters says,

> There is no post-missions era in the New Testament for the time of the church. To the contrary, the very commission which has loosened and sent thousands of men and women into the world with the gospel of Jesus Christ does not permit us to accept a post-missions era [1971:50].

Since Christian missions is God's own work, not some flimsy human enterprise, only a lack of faith and biblical insight can be at the root of such pessimism.

For another thing, this mentality is very ethnocentric. Just because the West is retreating as a colonial power and we may be entering into a post-*Western* age, in no sense do these facts lead to the conclusion that Christianity is retreating or that we are entering a post-*Christian* age. This reflects the distasteful colonial attitude of identifying Christianity with the West. It projects the unhealthy symptoms of many churches in the West upon Third World churches. Such negative thinking can be devastating to missionary strategy. Statements like the following can hardly contribute to the morale needed to fulfill the plan of God in the world:

> No matter how full of faith and optimism our missionary vision may be, we face the fact that, at our present rate of progress, there is no hope of the world ever being evangelized. It is estimated that not two percent of the world's population today are believing Christians . . . the proportion of heathenism, instead of showing any decrease, is steadily increasing against us [Hay 1947:16].

It is well known that a given set of data can be interpreted in more than one way. The needle of the gas tank in the car, for example, can be read "half empty" or "half full," depending on your frame of mind. Malcolm Forsberg of the Sudan Interior Mission advocates painting the encouraging side of the missionary picture. He says,

> Successful advertisers don't publicize the faults of their products, so why do Christians, especially missionaries, give in detail the story of their failures, mistakes and supposed lack of know-how in the Lord's work? [1968:2].

Alfred Krass, lamenting some present-day missionary attitudes, says, "We have made a virtue out of failure. We seem to thrive on people's lack of response" (1971:4).

The other side of the contemporary missions picture is given by Raymond Davis, also of the Sudan Interior Mission. He says,

> My approach is basically optimistic. This is not because of what I see or hear, but simply because I believe God is at work in the world and His program is precisely on schedule today as it ever has been and will be [1970:3].

In another statement, Davis also says, "Today is unmistakably the glorious, golden day of missions" (as quoted in Banks 1968:17). Davis' unbending faith in God and His promises allows him to interpret what he sees and hears in a positive and constructive way. There is undoubtedly a relationship between this attitude and the fact that the mission Davis leads is one of the largest and fastest-moving of all Interdenominational Foreign Missions Association missions.

Take Bible translation, for example. There are two ways of looking at this important ministry. The Wycliffe Bible Translators, generally speaking, stress the "two thousand tongues to go" side. On the other hand, the United Bible Societies stress the equally valid fact that the written Word of God is now available in the languages spoken by 97 percent of the world's population. While neither is false, they leave different impressions as to the present state of Bible translating ministry.

Anyone who reads Ralph Winter's *Twenty-Five Unbelievable Years;* David Barrett on Africa; Read, Monterroso, and Johnson on Latin America; or the myriad books rolling off the presses of the William Carey Library will know that, far from being a failure, Christian missions in the Third World are one of the most successful efforts of the day. George Peters "views missions as being in a time of unprecedented opportunity. This view is more scriptural (than the pessimistic view), factually more accurate, spiritually more uplifting, and historically more wholesome" (1971:50). McGavran has said that we are now only in the "sunrise of missions."

Even *U.S. News and World Report*, reporting on Barrett, seems to have had a change of heart from the pessimistic piece previously quoted. The lead paragraph in a recent article on Christianity in Africa reads: "The Christian faith may be in trouble in the Western world—but in Africa, it is growing more rapidly than ever" (1970:50).

Although the Red Chinese cloud has dimmed Asian missions somewhat, Asia also is participating in modern Christian ingathering. Warren Webster of the Conservative Baptist Foreign Mission Society has written recently:

> The political "retreat of the West" triggered an unfounded pessimism in some Christian circles. It lent false encouragement to critics who assumed that since western civilization and Christianity had spread hand in hand, they would both decline together. The opposite has taken place. With the exception of China and North Korea (which are in self-imposed isola-

tion), the church has gained strength and numbers in nearly every Asian country. . . . Strong Christian movements in South Korea and Indonesia have now grown to include nearly 10% of the population. . . . During the last twenty-five years, Christians in Taiwan have increased from 30,000 to 750,000. . . . In islands of the Pacific, 70-90% of the people of Oceania (outside New Guinea) have been discipled [1971: 15].

The power of positive missionary thinking is no myth. Living in the faith and expectation that the gates of hell are not going to prevail against the church is part of faithfulness to God. Many create self-fulfilling prophecies by lamenting over what God is not doing. Don Hillis once called this "spiritual flagellation" and confessed that his own participation in it "was far more an evidence of pride than of humility" (1968:9). This gloomy state of mind can blind us not only to what God is really doing in the world but also to what God wishes to do in the future. Good missionary strategy has rejected undue pessimism. It is filled with faith, optimism, and confidence in the power and victory of the Holy Spirit.

4

The Human Ingredient: Gifts and Call

IN THE FINAL ANALYSIS, missionary strategy is people. Since God, as we have seen, has chosen to use regenerated men and women to accomplish His evangelistic goals, one of our responsibilities is to analyze this human ingredient in missionary work. The recognition of the importance of the human ingredient in no way is intended to negate the supreme and ultimate role of the Holy Spirit in the mission of the church. But the better we understand the process that the Holy Spirit uses to make missionaries out of empty vessels fit for the Master's use, the better we will be able to deal with one another in our common attempt to fulfill the Great Commission.

Biblical teaching on spiritual gifts and especially their relationship to the missionary call is the most important element of a full-orbed understanding of the human element in missions.

BIBLICAL ASPECTS OF SPIRITUAL GIFTS

The scriptural norm for the doctrine of spiritual gifts is found in 1 Corinthians 12-14. Paul begins this key passage by writing, "Now concerning spiritual gifts, brethren, I would not have you ignorant." God wants us to understand what spiritual gifts are all about, and this furnishes an excellent starting point in defining what *missionary* really means and in relating it to the missionary call.

IDENTIFYING THE SPIRITUAL GIFTS

Every person who is a Christian has been "baptized into Christ's body" (1 Co 12:13). As a member of that body, he has been given one or more spiritual gifts which determine what function he should have in the body, also known as the church. Under Christ as the head, every member should be functioning properly by using his spiritual gift. This function must be coordinated with the other members of the body.

This is what Paul is talking about when he tells the Romans that no one should think too highly of himself, but that he should "think soberly [realistically], according as God hath dealt to every man the measure of faith" (Ro 12:3). As Paul goes on to explain in the passage, this "measure of faith" is another expression for the "gifts differing according to the grace that is given to us" (v. 6). These are distributed to every Christian without exception by the Holy Spirit. Some Christians may have multiple gifts, others only one, but all are expected to use whatever gifts they do have for the glory of God and for the benefit of the body as a whole.

The three key lists of the specific gifts are in 1 Corinthians 12 (two lists), Romans 12, and Ephesians 4. A synthesis of all the lists, combining gifts which in all probability refer to the same function, looks like this: apostleship, prophecy, teaching, evangelism, pastor, ministry, administration, wisdom, knowledge, faith, exhortation, miracles, healing, tongues, interpretation of tongues, discerning of spirits, giving, and mercy. Celibacy is mentioned as a gift in 1 Corinthians 7:7, and perhaps 1 Corinthians 13:3 would indicate that martyrdom should be added to the list.

These twenty gifts are just about all that are mentioned by name in the New Testament. However, this does not mean that any gifts not mentioned in these lists do not exist. The very fact that no list is complete in itself and some gifts are mentioned apart from the lists would lead us to conclude that since none of the parts is complete, the sum is not necessarily complete either. This is an important point, because later we are going to suggest that the "missionary gift" ought to be added to the list, even though this is not specifically mentioned in the Bible.

Spiritual gifts are not the same as natural talents, although Scripture does not make a particular point of the distinction. An unsaved person does not have any spiritual gifts, although he may have an abundance of natural talents. When he becomes a Christian, he then receives one or more spiritual gifts as his particular assignment as a new member of the body. Later on, the Holy Spirit may see fit to give him additional gifts. It may be that there is a close relationship between the spiritual gift that a person receives after conversion and the natural talents he had before. But again there may not be any connection at all, as would be the case with such gifts as tongues and prophecy. Spiritual gifts always relate to the functioning of the body of Christ, but natural talents may be used entirely separate from it.

RECOGNIZING THE SPIRITUAL GIFTS

The parable of the talents in Matthew 25 gives us an excellent indication of what God expects us to do with the spiritual gifts He has given us. Using financial investments as an illustration, Jesus teaches that whether a person receives five, two, or only one talent (read it as "gift"), he is expected to put it to active use, not to bury it. Good and faithful servants multiply their gifts. The final reckoning will come at the judgment seat of Christ. Note that in the parable, success and failure are carefully and statistically measured. Typically, whereas it takes fourteen words to report success, it takes forty-two words to report failure!

Each Christian will be held fully responsible for the profitable use of the gifts he has and for the results they produce. At the same time, it should be stressed that he will *not* be held accountable for the gifts he does not have. The servant with two talents is not responsible for the use of five.

One of the top priorities of the Christian life ought to be for each person to discover what spiritual gift he has so he can get on with the business of using it. Tragically, ignorance of spiritual gifts is widespread among Christians in general and missionaries in particular. Many have not taken the time in prayer and heart-searching necessary to reach an assurance of what their spiritual gifts are and what they are not. As a result, some people with spiritual gifts are not using them at all, while other people are futilely attempting jobs for which they have no gift and therefore are wasting their time. Little wonder the body of Christ often does not function as the Lord really wants it to.

When the body is functioning properly, all the gifts are in evidence and in dynamic use through the power of the Spirit of God. It must be remembered that the body of Christ is universal, with many local manifestations. Spiritual gifts are given to the body universal, and therefore certain ones may or may not be found in any particular local part of the body. This explains why, for example, a local church or even an entire denomination may not have been given the gift of tongues, while other parts of the body might have it. Gifts should never produce pride, nor should lack of gifts cause envy. God has fashioned the body properly, distributing the gifts as He wills (1 Co 12:11).

COORDINATING THE SPIRITUAL GIFTS

Spiritual gifts never can be used properly apart from the body as a whole. God expects His children to serve Him in the overall context of the church, with Christ at the head. A hand removed from the arm is of no use at all to any part of the body. This is one theological reason why independent missionary work often enjoys only minimal success.

As the head of the body, Christ coordinates the gifts and makes sure they are well used. He controls the central nervous system, and therefore all the gifts should function harmoniously together. If in certain cases they don't, it is usually because some member of the body lacks proper contact with the head.

Missionaries need to remember that they are members of a body. As such they cannot be indifferent to the other members. When one member rejoices, they all rejoice; when one member suffers, they all suffer. "The eye cannot say unto the hand, I have no need of thee" (1 Co 12:21). Failure to put these principles into practice is the cause for a great deal of unfruitful missionary work and should be corrected.

THE SOURCE OF SPIRITUAL GIFTS

All spiritual gifts are given by the Holy Spirit, and only by Him. God has chosen to reserve this responsibility for Himself without human aid. Neither theological seminaries nor church boards nor mission directors have the power to give gifts. They are responsible to help other Christians stir up their gifts, develop them in every way possible, and see that opportunities are provided for their use. But they cannot decide who will have this gift or who will have that one.

A Christian may desire to have a certain gift (1 Ti 3:1), but this does not assure him that he will get it. The passages which say "covet earnestly the best gifts" (1 Co 12:31) and "desire spiritual gifts" (1 Co 14:1) are collective commands relating not to individuals but to the Christian community as a whole. In other words, it is correct to want the body to have all the parts necessary for smooth operation.

Once we realize that the distribution of spiritual gifts is the exclusive responsibility of the Holy Spirit, we come to recognize that we have no ground for pride in what He has given us. Having a particular spiritual gift is in no sense a reward for some good deed, but it is given quite apart from any human effort. By the same token there is no room for envy on the part of one who perhaps has not been given as spectacular a gift as his brother. Envying the gifts of another really amounts to criticizing the Holy Spirit.

A common error in some Christian circles is to develop that false sense of humility which says, "I simply don't have any gifts. I'm just a nobody in the kingdom of God." Besides showing a lack of understanding of the Scriptures, this attitude is the shortest road toward burying the talent. It is not humility but disobedience. The final outcome may be the accusation of being a "wicked and slothful servant."

DISTINGUISHING GIFTS FROM FRUIT

The "more excellent way" than the gifts of the Spirit is the fruit of the Spirit (1 Co 12:31). The reason for this is that none of the spiritual gifts can operate properly without the simultaneous manifestation of the fruit of the Spirit: love, joy, peace, longsuffering, and the rest. This is why it was necessary for Paul to insert the chapter on love, the supreme fruit of the Spirit, right in the heart of the central passage on gifts, 1 Corinthians 12-14.

Unlike the gifts, the fruit of the Spirit is to be evident in the lives of *all* Christians. Whereas the gift of pastor may be given to only certain members of the body, love is expected from everyone without exception. Inward sanctification is seen outwardly by the fruit of the Spirit appearing in the life of the believer. However, no direct relationship between sanctification and the *possession* of spiritual gifts exists. Both carnal and spiritual Christians can and will *possess* spiritual gifts. But sanctification does have an important bearing on the *exercise* of the gifts. A carnal Christian can have gifts galore; but without the fruit of the Spirit, they are sounding brass and tinkling cymbal. This was one of the major problems in the Corinthian church. They had many gifts but little fruit. The value of their spiritual gifts was consequently nullified.

LOCATING THE "MISSIONARY GIFT"

Since the word *missionary* does not appear in any of the lists of spiritual gifts, the task of locating the "missionary gift" is not as simple as that of teaching or administration or healing. As a matter of fact, *missionary* is not a biblical term at all. For this reason a great deal of confusion has been generated over the matter of defining the word *missionary*.

A recent exchange of ideas on the subject in *Evangelical Missions Quarterly* surfaced a good many contrasting ideas. Representative of the hazy thinking on the part of many contemporary churchmen was a letter from pastor David Black. He expressed his own frustrations in this way:

> The more I read "missionary" literature and examine the work of "missionary" societies, the more confused I am about the meaning of "missionary." Why is a Christian college in Africa a "missionary" project, but a Christian college in the USA is not? Why are Christian doctors who go to a foreign country considered "missionaries" but not the ones who stay in the USA? Why are evangelists in the USA called "evangelists" but in foreign countries called "missionaries?" [1970: 191].

Black's provocative questions were subsequently answered by four letters and one full-length article. Samuel Rowen, who wrote the article, asks, "Should we drop the term 'missionary'?" He goes on to make the interesting classification of the organizational definition (identification with a missionary society), the cultural definition (cross-cultural communication), and the theological or biblical definition (every kingdom calling). After admitting some difficulty in making a practical distinction between the cultural and the theological definitions, Rowen suggests that "it may be appropriate that the term should be applied only to those called to kingdom service who are led to minister across cultural boundaries." But failing in this, "it may be time to reverse history and drop the term completely" (1971:97).

History probably will prove to be a little more stubborn than that. Words have a way of becoming rather permanent pieces of the mental furniture of individuals and communities. In spite of being little understood and extrabiblical, the term *missionary* is likely to be used widely in Christian circles for some time to come. Wishful thinking on the part of missionary theorists will not alter this fact of life. Therefore, the best approach is not to scrub the word but rather to come to a mutual agreement as to what we mean by it.

Probably the cultural definition is the most generally accepted among evangelical missiologists. Missionaries are Christian workers who engage in cross-cultural ministries with evangelistic goals. There is little doubt that this is what most knowledgeable people mean when they say "missionary." If so, how does it relate to what has been said about spiritual gifts? In order to answer this question, we will begin with some broad concepts and narrow them down toward the "missionary gift."

WITNESS AS A COMMON CHRISTIAN RESPONSIBILITY

All Christians are expected to witness, to share the gospel, and to lead others to Christ. There are no exceptions. Baseball provides a close parallel in that all nine players are expected to hit. Each must take a turn at bat.

But all baseball players do not have equal hitting ability. Many could never bat "clean up," but they are on the team because they make their major contribution in other ways, such as pitching or fielding. Similarly, all Christians do not have that special gift of evangelist which gives them extraordinary power in personal or public evangelism. Those with this gift regularly see bountiful results from their ministry. Since this gift of evangelist is given by the Holy Spirit only to certain members of the body of Christ, it would be well to call them evangelists and refer to the rest of the members of the body as witnesses. Everyone is a witness, but not everyone is an evangelist.

This distinction applies to other gifts as well. Liberality, for example, is mentioned as one of the spiritual gifts (Ro 12:8). Generosity in giving of one's income, at least a tenth and in many cases more, is a responsibility binding on every Christian. The Bible makes it a Christian virtue. But scattered throughout the body of Christ are those exceptional individuals who give an extraordinary proportion of their income to the Lord's work. They do this because the Spirit has given them the gift of liberality, and they are using it to God's glory.

By the law of averages, most Christians will lack more gifts than they have. In the very process of giving certain gifts to a Christian, the Holy Spirit withholds other gifts from him. The majority of Christians, for example, do not have the gifts of evangelist or liberality, in spite of the fact that they witness and give. By the same token, most Christians do not have the gift of missionary; nor should they.

This is why it is not accurate to say, as do some, "Every Christian must either go as a missionary or find a substitute." Paul Rees once reacted to this statement by commenting, "I am persuaded that the picture that is conjured up by such a sentence—a Christian man scurrying around to find a proxy who will function for him in mission—is essentially false" (1968*b*: 48). Every Christian is a witness, but not every Christian is a missionary. The missionary gift involves a *special kind* of witness.

CASUAL VERSUS STRUCTURED WITNESS

Casual witness occurs in the normal interpersonal relationships of daily life which bring a Christian into contact with such non-Christians as relatives, friends, and acquaintances. All Christians must take advantage of any opportunities to share Christ that this contact affords, attempting to persuade others to become Christians. In order to do this, no spiritual gift is needed; all good Christians do it. Therefore, the search for the "missionary gift" cannot be located among those who participate in casual witness.

Structured witness is something again. This requires a certain planning and investment of resources in the evangelization of a certain community. It also requires spiritual gifts. As a matter of fact, only those who have appropriate gifts should participate. Missionaries work in a structured witnessing situation rather than a casual one. But others, such as professional evangelists and pastors, do also. This brings us closer to the identity of a missionary, but we still need to make a finer distinction.

CALLED VERSUS SENT WITNESS

Within structured witnessing situations, some are called and some are sent. By *called* we refer to the action of a church or other representative of the Christian community, in contrast to the more theologically-oriented meaning of the call of God first to salvation and then to service.

Some members of the body of Christ who have gifts of evangelist, pastor, or teacher are often called to minister to a certain group. The group which calls him assumes responsibility for his job description, his finances, and his accountability. In the case of a pastor, for example, he can be called to a church in his own country or in a different country, but he is still *called* rather than *sent*. The same thing applies to an evangelist. In other words, moving from one country to another in a "called" ministry does not make a person a missionary. When British pastor Alan Redpath was called to pastor the Moody Church in Chicago, he was not considered a British missionary to the United States, but simply a British pastor ministering in the United States. Likewise, Billy Graham was not considered a missionary when he recently held a campaign in Germany. This clarification helps our definition of missionary, since it shows that crossing geographical boundaries does not, ipso facto, make a person a missionary.

On the other hand, the person who is sent out rather than

called is much closer to what we do mean by the word *missionary*. The word itself comes from the Latin root, *missio*, which always carries the connotation of sending off. Missionary is not a biblical word, but the biblical Greek term nearest to it is probably *apostolos*, which has the same connotation of being sent. In the *Living New Testament*, Ken Taylor regularly translates *apostolos* as "missionary," although this may be slightly too close a connection. It all ties in, however, with the way most Americans understand the word *missionary*, according to the unabridged *Random House Dictionary:* "A missionary is a person sent by a church into an area, especially into a newly-settled region or foreign country, to carry on evangelism or other activities."

A missionary is a person who engages in a structured rather than a casual witnessing situation and who is sent to his ministry rather than called to it.

THE THREE KINDS OF MISSIONARIES

Added to the characteristics already described, the missionary, as the term is understood, also has some sort of cross-cultural involvement.

Writing in *Evangelical Missions Quarterly*, Ralph Winter proposes a threefold classification of missionaries, which may turn out to be one of the most helpful new thoughts on the subject in many a day. He labels the groups M_1, M_2, and M_3 missionaries (1970:55).

An M_1 missionary carries on an intracultural ministry. He is sent, as are other missionaries, but to peoples whose language and culture do not differ significantly from his own. He does not need to learn a new language. He does not pass through a traumatic culture shock. At the same time, he may travel halfway around the globe. A United States seminary graduate, for example, might be sent out by his Presbyterian church to minister to the American community in Caracas, Venezuela. A Japanese evangelist might be sent out by his Methodist church in Tokyo to evangelize the Japanese colonists in Brazil. A Baptist church in one of Kinshasa's growing suburbs might send a man over to the other side of town to plant a church among people of the same tribe who have settled in a different suburb. All these are M_1 missionaries.

An M_2 missionary carries on an interdialectal ministry. He learns a foreign language, but the linguistic and cultural differences between the second culture and his own are minimal. Missionaries sent from England to France or the cities of Brazil or Mexico City are M_2 missionaries. Cross-cultural involvement is there, but it is minimal.

An M_3 missionary carries on an intercultural ministry in the most radical sense. He is sent to minister to people whose language and culture are entirely strange to him. The language contains no cognate words, and it might even have exotic tonal variations. Examples of this would include a missionary from Germany to the Campas of Peru, the Vietnamese, or the Arabs of Jordan. To minimize the geographical factor, this would include also a United States missionary to the Navajos of his own country.

WHICH MISSIONARIES HAVE THE "GIFT"?

No particular missionary gift is needed for an M_1 missionary. Travel in itself doesn't mean that much. If the worker's hometown is Miami, for example, his ministry among Americans in Caracas would actually mean *less* travel than if he were called to a church in Seattle. The cross-cultural factor in Caracas is at best marginal, and in some cases the called-sent distinction could even be neutralized if the church in Venezuela calls him as pastor. In other cases, however, the sent factor is the one which causes people to think of most M_1 missionaries as missionaries. A schoolteacher from the United States, for example, may hear of a need in a missionary children's school in India and be sent there to teach by her home church. In spite of the fact that no cross-cultural ministry is involved, she is sent out to associate with a missionary community in India. Organizationally, then, she is a missionary and undoubtedly will be called such by her friends in spite of all that mission theorists might say. The fact remains, however, that what we are calling the "missionary gift" is not required for her.

It is required, however, for the M_2 and M_3 missionary. They must be enabled by God to minister cross-culturally effectively. The ministry might involve the use of any other spiritual gift the person might have. He might be an evangelist, a teacher, a helper, an administrator, or have any other function in the body of Christ. If he has the ability to make profitable use of that gift in a cross-cultural situation, he has, by definition, the "missionary gift." It has been mentioned that not all Christians have the missionary gift. Those who do not would be well advised to use the gifts they *do* have in their own cultures, because if they try a cross-cultural ministry without this necessary spiritual equipment, they probably will fail. This, I believe, is the theological explanation for what some call "missionary casualties."

Missionary casualties should not be blamed personally for not having the missionary gift. We have seen already that the Holy Spirit gives or withholds these gifts from Christians, and His will in the matter should be respected. But it is a serious Christian responsibility for each one to *discover* the gifts he has as well as those he doesn't have. If this spiritual exercise were more of a part of our normal church life, we undoubtedly would see fewer missionary casualties.

Some may object at this point by saying that the missionary gift is not mentioned in any of the New Testament lists. This is true, but we have seen also that there is no reason to believe that either the separate lists or the synthesis of them is exhaustive. The term *missionary* is simply a useful way of designating a kind of person the Holy Spirit has been using in the church through the years in a function that had not become particularly evident when the New Testament was written.

Especially in Roman Catholic missiology, as well as in the *Living New Testament* and other Protestant writings, a tendency to make an exact equivalent between the gift of "apostle" and the "missionary gift" is evident. Etymologically there is a close relationship, and in ministry there might be much similarity also. But it does seem that the concept of apostleship in the New Testament involves both more and less than the missionary gift implies. An apostle is more than a missionary because he has a certain God-given authority among a particular group of churches which some missionaries who are not

apostles might lack. An apostle is less than a missionary because he does not necessarily need a gift for cross-cultural
communication, as the apostle Peter illustrates. (In spite of all,
he was never quite able to identify himself with the Gentiles.)
    The missionary gift never stands alone. God gives it to sup-
plement whatever other gifts a particular Christian may have.
In order to be an effective missionary, the person must already
have gift X, and also the missionary gift so that he will be
able to use gift X cross-culturally. If a person has gift X but
not the missionary gift, he should use his gift X, but in his
own culture. If God wanted him to minister with it in another
culture, He would have given him the missionary gift.
    An example of lack of sensitivity to the missionary gift has
occurred in the United States, where the black community has
not been adequately recognized as a separate subculture. It
has been very difficult for white seminaries to excel in training
black leaders. Why? Part of the answer probably lies in the
fact that, although the white seminary professors have the gift
of teaching, they do not have the missionary gift necessary to
handle the cross-cultural situation caused by black culture in
which the student hopes to minister when he graduates. In
order to pass the course he probably will have to learn to
preach like a white man.
    This, of course, is not only true of white seminaries in the
United States, but also of many others around the world where
multicultural situations exist. Quechuas will find the same
problem in middle-class schools in Ecuador. Taiwanese hill
people struggle with it in Chinese seminaries. Wherever a
significant cultural gap can be discerned, a requirement for
people who cross it should be the missionary gift.

SOME PRACTICAL APPLICATIONS

    Up to now, this chapter has dealt largely with theoretical
considerations of spiritual gifts and how missionaries fit into
the picture. There are many areas of practical application
which should be mentioned before concluding this discussion.
Perhaps the best place to begin is to apply them to what is
known as the "missionary call."

THE MISSIONARY CALL

The recent book *Christian Collegians and Foreign Missions* (Barkman et al., 1969) reveals that, at least among North American Christian college students, a good bit of confusion exists as to just what the missionary call is. Even missionaries themselves are unclear. The Urbana survey showed that "missionaries vary little from delegates [students] in their view of whether a missionary call is a special call, splitting 57 to 43 in favor of its not being a special call" (Ibid.:144).

Partly to offset this problem, David Howard wrote a widely circulated pamphlet entitled, *Don't Wait for the Macedonians,* in which he said,

> The idea of a "call" has been so overworked that it is a small wonder if someone gets hung-up on it. While it is a biblical word . . . it has too often become a meaningless cliche. Perhaps this is partly because we have failed to discern what the Bible really means when it speaks of a "Call" [1970*b*:n.p.].

With few exceptions, missionary literature does not stress the relationship between the missionary call and the spiritual gifts. This is a major reason for the confusion. One of the few mission executives who have written on this important matter is Dick Hillis of Overseas Crusades. He says, "I believe your calling and gift are identical. Your call is what you are to be, which is determined by the gift He has given you" (n.d.,n.p.).

If college students and others could see clearly the biblical fact that the gift and the call go hand in hand, they would be more likely to be able to discern God's will for them concerning missionary service. God never gives a call without giving the gift or gifts necessary to fulfill the call. Conversely, God never gives a gift without calling the person who has it to use that gift for His glory. This principle is no different when applied to the missionary gift than when applied to any other spiritual gift.

Specifically how does this work?

God first gives the missionary gift to those whom He chooses. Then He expects each one who receives it to recognize the fact that he has it and that he will use it for God's glory.

For many young people, this is not an easy thing to discern.

If a person has not even traveled to another culture, he may need some special and subjective assurance beforehand that he has the missionary gift. Before the days of jet travel, most missionaries went to the foreign field with no previous experience or contact with another culture. The ones who stayed on probably had correctly discerned that internal leading of God. Many of those who failed may have confused other feelings and inclinations with the voice of God and found out that they did not have the gift, only after arriving on the field and trying in vain to make the cross-cultural adjustment.

Modern missionary recruiting should learn from the past and be geared toward separating the applicants who have the missionary gift from those who do not. No system will ever be completely accurate at this point, but an attempt to approach the goal should be made. Some homelands afford the opportunity for cross-cultural involvement without much travel. The current trend for short-term involvement in missionary work abroad is also an excellent opportunity for young people to get some early indication as to whether they have the missionary gift.

By the time a person recognizes that God has given him the missionary gift, he also should have discovered what other gift or gifts he is expected to use for the kingdom of God. At this point, a decision is needed to use these gifts, whatever the cost may be. This is the step of *missionary commitment*, presenting one's body a living sacrifice. It is coming into a conscious willingness to obey God in a personal way. Sometimes the whole process involved in this volitional act is labeled a missionary call. In a sense it is a misnomer; but whatever word is used, it is a crucial point in the Christian life.

In many cases, Christian people never reach this step of commitment to the use of their spiritual gifts because they have not been taught to recognize their spiritual gifts in the first place. This indicates a deficiency in evangelical pastoral care, which should be corrected.

Naturally, the individual Christian is not left to himself. Besides the ministry of the Holy Spirit directly in his own life, he also benefits from the action of the whole body of Christ. If a person really has the gifts of the Spirit he thinks he has, the church will confirm this as a group. One missionary candidate I know has this confirmed already. A northern white, he has become a well-adjusted and accepted assistant pastor of an all-black church in the southern United States, while finishing his theological preparation. Before leaving for the mission field, the body of Christ in the homeland has confirmed his missionary gift.

Recognition of the gifts, commitment to their use, and confirmation by the church are important milestones in Christian service. Following this, the gifts should be developed by all means that are available. This is what Bible institutes and seminaries are really designed for, although it is true that many of the students in them had no mature assurance of what gifts they might have had when they enrolled. If a person has the gift of teacher, for example, he should develop it by studying pedagogy and theology. The missionary gift should be developed by systematically studying the language and culture of the people who will receive him. One who has the gift of administrator should keep up on the latest developments in the fields of management and planning. God expects each one of His servants to be the best steward possible of whatever gifts he has been given.

The final step in applying the missionary call is the decision as to where. But in reality, the matter of the geographical location of where the missionary gift finally will be used is a secondary one. If we can use the apostle Paul as an example (in spite of the fact that he was an M_1 missionary), we find that he received his basic calling to missionary work through Ananias: "He is a chosen vessel unto me, to bear my name before the Gentiles, and kings, and the children of Israel" (Ac 9:15). The first time the Scripture gives an indication of a definite *geographical* leading comes in Paul's second term when the Spirit turns him away from Bithynia and Asia and sets him on the road to Macedonia (Ac 16:6-9). But while Paul did have a "Macedonian vision," we are not told that he had a "Berean vision" or a "Corinthian vision." Rather than giving specific visions for each phase of Paul's missionary work, the Holy Spirit led him into sound strategy and planning, as we have seen in chapter 2.

It is probably true that the missionary gift will enable a person to minister cross-culturally in any second culture. This does not mean that it is wrong for a missionary to dedicate his life to only one second culture, but it does mean that he could probably adapt equally well to a third culture, if God so led him into a harvest field there.

"EVERY CHRISTIAN A MISSIONARY"

I recently heard a young missionary say, "We all know that everyone is a missionary and that the mission field is everywhere." I do not blame him for saying this, because it is so frequently repeated in our evangelical churches and missionary conventions. It is, of course, highly inaccurate, just as much as saying "every Christian is a pastor" or saying the whole body is an eye (1 Co 12:17). Samuel Rowen reduced this concept to the absurd when he described an occasion when the student body of a Bible institute voted the staff of the school—cooks, maintenance men, and so forth—as the "forgotten missionaries" (1971:93).

This is an overly sentimental use of the word *missionary*. While it may be quite harmless to call the pastry chef in a monocultural institution a missionary, it does not help clarify the thinking of the young people who are studying there and struggling with the call of God in their own lives. The pastry chef could be called a faithful Christian worker or an effective witness for Christ, but please, not a missionary.

MISSIONARY AND EVANGELIST

In some circles the terms *missionary* and *evangelist* have been too closely identified. This is somewhat understandable, due to the fact that the basic goal of missionary work is evangelistic. But the evangelistic goals are accomplished by a body with many members, by a team of Christians. On the team, all M_2 or M_3 missionaries will have the missionary gift of ministering cross-culturally, but not all will have the gift of evangelist. Some might be missionary teachers; some might be missionary helpers; some might be missionary administrators. The distinguishing characteristic of a missionary is not therefore the gift of evangelist, but the missionary gift.

PLACEMENT STRATEGY

The processing and placement of missionary personnel should be based as much as possible on the principles of spiritual gifts. At times exceptions must be made for temporary assignments, but the goal of every mission administrator should be to place each missionary where he will enjoy the widest possible opportunities to make use of the gifts that God has given him.

This principle helps avoid the frustration produced in the person who is expected to do a certain job but fails at it because he does not have the necessary spiritual gift. Effective placement helps create in the mission family a sense of team accomplishment. One administrator of a school for missionaries' children was criticized recently because he was not leading enough souls to Christ. This was unfair because, in the first place, the critics had confused the gift of administration with that of evangelist, and, in the second place, the administrator was daily freeing scores of other missionaries to lead souls to Christ, who wouldn't have been nearly as effective in the use of their spiritual gifts if it weren't for the school. As every football fan knows, the offensive guards and tackles never score touchdowns, but their team couldn't win without them.

My own experience leads me to make a final statement. I think that the major reason for so-called missionary failures is the lack of the missionary gift. Somewhere spiritual signals got crossed, and the individual erroneously believed that God had "called" him to the mission field and had given him the necessary gifts. But after some time and expense spent in frustration and failure, it became quite evident that this was not the case; and the missionary went home for good. In most cases, this is not stated as clearly as it is here. The failure is often successfully camouflaged by promotional phrases. Other reasons are often presented for leaving the field, such as ill health, family needs in the homeland, children's education, or just "God's will." This is not to say that none of these can become a *legitimate* cause for someone who does have the missionary gift and has proved it successfully, to be forced to change his career. But it is to say that in many cases of younger missionaries not making the grade, the underlying cause may be located here. This is one reason why a crystal-clear doctrine of spiritual gifts, especially the place of the missionary gift, and call in the body of Christ is essential for the development of the best missionary strategy.

5

Bending Strategy to Fit Culture

ONE FACTOR that separates missionary strategy from many other kinds of strategy is that the cross-cultural element is of key importance. By definition, missionary work involves cross-cultural activity. In missions, therefore, strategy cannot be planned properly without first coming to terms with the theoretical and practical aspects of culture, culture shock, and culture overhang.

CULTURE—THE RULES OF THE GAME

It is helpful to think of culture in terms of being the rules of the game. The game, in this case, is human life and relationships; and culture is the set of rules which each particular group of human beings designs and mutually accepts as its own style of life. Wherever a cluster of human beings is found together, it is certain that they have a complex set of rules which they either obey or disobey, in which case they pay a penalty.

Cultural rules are not always easy to learn. In the case of basketball rules, one can buy a rule book, study it, and to a large extent master the rules. In case of doubt, right or wrong can be proved from the book. But the rule books of culture are largely unwritten; and they can be learned only by observation, experience, and trial and error.

Some cultural rules have been written down. They are usually called laws. England has a law which says that motorists must keep to the left, for example; and the United States has a similar one which requires motorists to keep to the right. This reflects an easily observable cultural difference. But even in highly advanced societies, the written laws comprise only a fraction of the cultural rules of the game; and the rest must

be learned by experience. There is no law which forces English-
men to hold their fork in the left hand, and Americans to hold
theirs in the right hand; but this is as much a part of culture
as the traffic patterns. And, of course, the world's illiterate
cultures have no written rules at all. No one has ever counted
the number of cultural rules in effect among a given people—
there may well be as many rules and nuances as words in the
vocabulary.

Sooner or later, the rules of a culture will touch every single
aspect of life. Although few people who have lived their whole
lives in only one culture realize its effects upon them, every
action throughout the day, and even the way one sleeps at
night, has been conditioned to one degree or another by cultural rules. From major life decisions, such as whom you
marry to whether you let your first child live rather than bury
it alive, down to the minor ones, like how you bathe or how
far you stand from the person you are conversing with, all are
predetermined by culture.

Cultures, like fingerprints, are all different. Even within one
nation, many different subcultures may exist side by side. In
the United States, for example, New Englanders live by some
cultural rules quite different from Southern Californians. But
in Southern California itself, there is one rule book for the
black community, one for the Chicanos, one for the hippies,
one for university students, and so on. True, many cultural
rules overlap from one group to another—for example, they all
drive on the right and use credit cards. But the differences are
significant enough to allow these groups to be classified anthro-
pologically as distinct subcultures. A well-tuned ear can even
listen to the English they speak and identify their cultural
background.

Naturally, some cultural rules are very obvious. It does not
take long for an outsider to discover that Chinese eat with chop
sticks, that Indian ladies dress in saris, and that Brazilians
speak Portuguese. But these are only surface indications, like
the small puddle of oil that gives a clue to vast deposits beneath
the surface. Specialists have been trained to observe and
describe cultural rules that the ordinary person would not see.
Some anthropologists, like Oscar Lewis, have had the ability

to communicate these patterns to others. Even after several years' experience in Latin America, I had not been able to pick up a fraction of the cultural insights that came from a reading of his book *The Children of Sánchez*. Missionaries whose business it is to understand other cultures should make every effort to supplement their own observation and experience with all available specialized studies.

Cultural rules of the game are programmed into children's minds like data is programmed into an electronic computer. This is the most natural and most effective way for a culture to be learned. We have all gone through the process, so we understand it to a degree. But when an adult, with his mind already programmed with his own set of cultural values, attempts to learn a new set of rules, he finds it much more difficult. This is the reason why, even if one has the missionary gift, perfection in linguistic or cultural adaptation is virtually unattainable. Missionaries should resign themselves to always being known and recognized as a gringo or Westerner, or whatever the others might call him.

As a personal experiment, anthropologist William Reyburn once tried to fool the Quechua Indians. His anthropological skills enabled him to neutralize the language and the dress as identifying factors. Nevertheless, other subtle clues gave him away; and wherever he went, the Quechuas called him *patrón* (boss). He later discovered that his walking stride was one of the tip-offs. But finally, when he asked one Quechua what the problem could be, he was told, "You don't have an Indian mother!" Nothing could have been more eloquent.

One of the most important tasks in planning missionary strategy is accurately to identify the cultures and subcultures of a given region. Political boundaries, such as in Africa, many times have been drawn with no sensitivity to cultural boundaries. When this is done, wars and international strife are inevitable. To a degree the Vietnam war was caused by cultural clashes between the north and south, two different peoples.

The assumption that all who live within a certain nation share the same culture has been an obstacle to sound missionary strategy in many cases. Personal observations have indicated that this fallacy is one of the clues as to why in Bolivia Aymaras have been won to Christ in large numbers, while the neighboring Quechuas have not been won to the same extent. Aymara speakers are in general culturally homogeneous. On the other hand the Quechuas, although they speak a common tongue, are culturally heterogeneous and divided into multiple subcultures. Premised on the erroneous assumption of cultural homogeneity, missionary work among the Quechuas has enjoyed relatively little success.

CULTURE SHOCK—LEARNING THE RULES

As we have mentioned, adult learning in a second culture is more difficult than learning culture as a child, because the mental computer has to be reprogrammed. This applies to culture in general, and in particular to that special element of culture that usually is the most difficult for missionaries to learn—language. Certain ingrained attitudes have to be erased before new data can be learned. For example, most monolingual Americans believe that the *correct* word for what I am sitting on is *chair*. This is a wrong attitude that must be unlearned. *Stuhl* or *silla* or *idabedabe* are all equally correct, in spite of the fact that they are different. Since such mistaken cultural attitudes have not been so deeply ingrained into children, they can much more readily absorb a second culture and language. Many missionary parents have experienced the phenomenon of seeing their children learn the language more rapidly than the grownups.

Most North American boys know the rules of baseball without remembering where and when they learned them. They all seem simple and even natural—until one attempts to explain them to an Englishman! Only when the American watches his first cricket match, does he, in turn, understand what the poor Englishman went through. These difficult cultural adaptations may be described as having "two strikes against you" or as a "sticky wicket," both good English language terms.

An unusual phenomenon involving missionary children might also be mentioned in passing. According to one theory, children of expatriates develop their own subcultural patterns on a transnational basis. If the parents come from culture A and the children are reared by them in culture B, their own cultural patterns will duplicate neither A nor B, but rather will form a C pattern. This means that a diplomat's son reared in Indonesia will have more in common with a missionary kid from Congo than he will with the average American or Indonesian. To a degree, missionaries themselves take on a C pattern after many years of service. On the field others say, "He's a foreigner; he really doesn't understand us." But at home they say, "He's a missionary; he's out of it."

All this explains why an adult who has to learn a new set of rules for his behavior in a second culture goes through a traumatic experience. We call this experience "culture shock."

There is nothing wrong with having culture shock. Per se, it is not pathological, although it can become pathological if not properly handled. If a Christian has the missionary gift, this means that he has a special ability to make the cultural transition and is likely to have a minimum of trauma. But even the missionary gift does not exempt a worker from culture shock of one degree or another.

International missions, which draw their personnel from more than one homeland, present new workers with a double culture shock situation. When British and American missionaries are working together on the same field, for example, mutual adjustment is not to be taken for granted. It is easy for an American to adjust to British customs in Great Britain, and likewise for an Englishman to adjust to American customs in the United States. But when the two meet each other on neutral territory, who yields? This is a potential powder keg, which only the ministry of the Holy Spirit can care for.

A third kind of emotional shock should also be mentioned. This is the often painful process of "dehaloizing" the missionaries. Usually older workers who arrive on the mission field at a late age feel this more acutely than do younger workers. It is easy to understand. Christians in the homelands who have seen missionaries only behind the pulpit or in their homes for a Sunday dinner or even in a week-long missionary conference are likely to fall into the trap of thinking that all missionaries wear halos. Just about any missionary can be on his best behavior for a day or a week and make no mistakes. But when new workers arrive on the field and begin to associate with missionaries in the normal give-and-take of daily life, they discover, much to their dismay, that missionaries are just as human as other servants of the Lord. Many are so shocked by this unexpected turn of events that they hastily conclude that missionaries are really *worse* than anyone else. It takes time for the pendulum to swing back into its proper place.

THE DOWNHILL ROAD OF CULTURE SHOCK

All who move into a second culture to live will find themselves on a downhill road of culture shock. Some successfully turn around and begin improvement before others. Some get down so far that they cannot make it back out of the depths. The four major steps downhill can be described as follows:

1. *The tourist stage.* When a person first arrives in a new country, especially after a long trip, he finds his surroundings quaint and exciting. *National Geographic* comes to life! A good deal of time is spent exploring and taking pictures. He pinches himself to make sure he is really there in the midst of such an exotic people. Real tourists never pass this stage, nor do they have to. The things they do not like make little difference because they soon will be heading home to "civilization." But when the new arrival is not a tourist, he soon will move down to the second step.

2. *Rejecting strange values.* Once it occurs to the new missionary that he is not soon going back to "civilization" and that he is in a new home, he is forced to begin to make value judgments about his surroundings. He sees many things which seem to him to violate the rules of life itself, and they offend him. Of course his rule book is quite different in many aspects from the rule book of the new culture, but he cannot yet see this objectively. He reacts negatively because people all around him are breaking his rules, and he feels they should either change or be punished for not changing. The dirt in the marketplace is *wrong*, changing governments by revolution rather than by elections is *wrong*, eating unhatched chicks is *wrong*, urinating in public is *wrong*, painting political slogans on the walls is *wrong* (especially when they say "Yankee Go Home").

The intensity of the rejection of strange cultural values will differ from person to person, but it carries some new missionaries quite far down the road of culture shock.

3. *Craving familiar values.* Rejection tends to *push* the culture-shocked person away from his new surroundings. A feeling of homesickness or a craving for familiar values and symbols of them will enter to reinforce this mental state and produce a *pull* factor. This may cause melancholy, daydreams, romantic illusions about the good old days at home, and some more uncomfortable symptoms. If all this is recognized as a rather common part of the process of cultural adjustment, it can be relatively harmless. If not, it can become dangerous. This kind of emotional disturbance can cause spiritual problems. The devil may use it to bring in such things as gossip, a loss of vision, twisted perspectives, envy, or a lack of vital touch with the Lord. A close walk with the Lord and full confidence in the ministry of the Holy Spirit are essential for victory at this crucial stage of missionary work.

Long-term observation of culture-shocked people has revealed certain identifiable symptoms which characterize some new arrivals (or even long-termers who have learned to live with perpetual culture shock rather than having recovered from it). They include hesitancy to leave the house, exclusive association with other missionaries or foreigners, unwillingness to hire a maid or use nationals as baby-sitters, obsession for washing the hands, disgust for national food and drink, distrust of national medical and dental service, excessive worry over being robbed or cheated, and of course constant criticism of the national way of life with unfavorable comparisons to the "way we do it back home."

4. *Depression.* This fourth stage is the pathological extreme of culture shock. Fortunately, not all reach it. In it, the culture-shocked person succumbs to defeat. Often he suffers physical symptoms from psychosomatic causes which are not recognized immediately as results of culture shock. Skillful therapy is needed for the small percentage of new missionaries who reach this stage. Many will respond to the therapy and emerge from their depression. Those who do not, in all probability, will do one of two things: (*a*) They will totally reject the sec-

ond culture and return to the first, or (*b*) they will overcompensate for their problem and "go native." The person who finds it necessary to take either one of these paths has reached the bottom of the culture shock hill and, in doing so, has proved by definition that he did not have the missionary gift.

THE UPHILL ROAD OF ADJUSTMENT

In general, the therapy needed to turn around and begin to pull out of culture shock involves imparting to the new worker a feeling of love and belonging, a sense of humor, and an intelligent evaluation of what is happening to him during this process. The very reading of a chapter like this is all the therapy that many will need. If the problem itself is adequately understood and identified, the effects are diminished.

As has been mentioned, Satan will attempt to use culture shock as an instrument to destroy the new worker. This underscores the vital importance of the spiritual dimension. Special diligence in the practice of piety, a steady devotional life, much time in prayer, and a deliberate appropriation of the presence of the Holy Spirit are needed even more than in other phases of life.

Practical and positive steps should be taken by those who are suffering from culture shock. The following, somewhat in this order, have been found helpful to many.

1. Take an active interest in discovering and defining the differences between the two cultures. Observation, reading, and discussion with older, more experienced workers will help. Avoid unfavorable comparisons to your homeland. You will begin to see the new rules of the cultural game more clearly in contrast to your old rules.

2. Make a conscious effort to detach yourself from the old culture. In order to do this, you must realize that all cultures are relative and that in no sense is your old culture any more *right* than the new one. Accept it as different but not better.

3. Develop the ability to communicate with those from the new culture. Until you can understand the signs along the streets and what people are trying to say to you, you will remain culture-shocked. All missions recognize the importance of language learning and make provision for their new workers.

But the language learning per se is often not enough. William Wonderly points out that languages usually have four spoken styles, the *formal*, which is the dress-up way the language is "supposed" to be spoken; the *regular*, which is the normal speech used between relative strangers; the *casual*, used between friends and which assumes that the other possesses certain information that need not be repeated; and the *intimate*, used not so much to exchange information as to convey feelings. Many missionaries have reduced their effectiveness in communication because they never have developed their language skills past formal and regular speech. Wonderly recommends that missionaries make a concerted effort to master the casual style of speech:

> This is especially important in the context of the modern missionary movement, in which the missionary no longer plays the role of an administrator and overseer with whom the use of a more formal style is felt to be fitting. . . .
>
> If he does not he forces other people either to use regular and formal style in his presence or to become irked at his failure to understand their own casual give and take [1966: 101].

4. Develop independence in your life and movement. Force yourself to move out of the foreign ghetto both physically and socially, even though you may feel much more comfortable in it. By not doing this, many businessmen and diplomats seal themselves off from the people of the second culture. Missionaries, however, do not have the option of forming a cultural ghetto, since they have been sent with the express purpose of identifying with and ministering to the people in a personal way. One of the obvious disadvantages of a mission compound or even a missionary guest home is that they tend to create ghettos which can work against good missionary strategy.

5. Understand the people you are working with and develop an empathy for them. This involves not only knowing what their rules are but understanding why those particular rules are helpful. Some missionaries to Bolivia thought it was ridiculous to have to back a car uphill and around a curve in order to get a driver's license. But on their first trip through the

Andes on the narrow dirt roads where the law requires that, when two vehicles meet, the one going downhill has to back up until the other can pass, they understood why. Most missionaries are offended by the cultural pattern of polygamy they find in Africa. But some recent analyses of this situation have suggested that perhaps a rereading of the Old Testament and the way it confronted similar cultural values may warrant a more lenient policy than some missions have established. Anthropologists have long pointed out that some excellent cultural considerations underly the practice.

6. Personally appropriate for yourself the new culture in every way possible (not polygamy!). Once you learn and understand the rules, practice them. If the people around you are living well-adjusted lives under their cultural rules, with a little effort you can do so also. In time, it will be fun. Your culture shock will be over. You will fit, and others will recognize that you are fitting well. Since your habits will be meaningful to the people, you will find them in turn warmer and more apt to receive the message of the gospel.

BENEFITS OF CURED CULTURE SHOCK

Like any healthy learning experience, mastering a new set of rules for the game of life is an enriching experience. Those who have successfully passed through a period of culture shock emerge different people, in many ways healthier and better adjusted. They have had an advantage that monocultural people are denied.

For one thing, the culture shock experience produces a deeper sense of human values. It helps a person shed the ethnocentrism which tends to give him an extremely nearsighted and provincial view of the world. The new expansiveness that adaptation to a second culture produces in the personality helps him to see the broader picture of God's work in the world. Those who have been confined to the Western world, for example, often have fallen into the erroneous assumption that mankind is in a post-Christian age, simply a reflection of their own ethnocentrism. Few missionaries who have participated in the work of God in the Third World would share their point of view.

Once a person appropriates a second culture, he earns the freedom to look back and make some constructive criticisms of his former values. Don Hillis once said,

> I thank God for taking me out of affluent America and placing me in hungry India. . . . My years in India removed from me any desire to cling to a stockpile of material blessings [1968:6].

When the first case of culture shock is cured, one finds that he is practically immune to further serious cases. He has developed a healthy self-confidence that will aid him in any number of crises in life. When he moves to a third or fourth culture, he will find that his attitudes toward the cultural rules of the game have changed to the point that the adjustment is not only easier but a pleasing experience.

CULTURAL OVERHANG—CHANGING THE RULES

Just as culture shock is universally present in cross-cultural adaptation, so is cultural overhang. To one degree or another, no one who moves to a second culture is able to shed his old skin completely. Deep in the heart of man, even in missionaries, lurks that "creator complex" by which he delights in making other people over in his own image. Since we find it more difficult to play the game of life by a new set of rules, we are continually tempted to try to convince other people that they should play by *our* rules. How much easier it would be if the Aucas would learn English, rather than making us learn Auca. If only Latin Americans could learn to get to appointments on time!

While we might not be able to rid ourselves completely of cultural overhang, we can take steps to reduce it; and the more we succeed in this effort the more effective our ministry will be.

The first and most important step is to recognize the fact that cultural overhang is present and potentially dangerous. Many times this is even more difficult because our interpretation of certain biblical passages has been conditioned by our culture, and we are not even aware of it. This places us in the difficult situation of identifying certain cultural values with the will of God. Some of the more frequent examples of this have been the assumptions that the Bible itself teaches that democracy is the ideal political form and that capitalism is the ideal economic system. As most Third World intellectuals will soon inform you, this is a highly questionable hermeneutic.

As much as possible we should resist our inherent desire to dominate others or to impose upon them our cultural standards. I recently read that the people of New Guinea believed so strongly in equality that, when the children learned to play soccer, the games always ended in a tie. But the foreign teachers persisted until the children finally learned how to play to win. The foreign cultural value was thereby imposed upon the children. But is there anything inferior about equality as a cultural value? Many say that we in the United States need more, not less, of this quality.

Speaking of children, one of the most disliked aspects of cultural overhang is treating the people of the second culture like children. This is called paternalism. When we fail to recognize that adults of a different culture are adults in their own right and that to them much of *our* behavior seems childish, we ooze a disgusting superiority complex which is a serious stumbling block to purposeful communication.

Cultural paternalism is extremely ethnocentric. At times it manifests itself in the desire to be the appreciated benefactor. In Latin America, for example, it is not the custom to open a gift until the giver leaves. Some North Americans, unaware of this, have insisted that the recipient go through the painful (for him) process of opening the gift and thanking the giver on the spot. At that point the Latin certainly understands that it is more blessed to give than to receive, and very often embarrassment is produced because he has nothing equivalent to give in return. He would rather have received no gift at all, but he hides these feelings under a surface veneer. This is one reason why United States foreign aid often produces resentment in the long run rather than friendship. Even much ecclesiastical aid to foreign churches carries with it the requirement of "accountability," which may well be a disguised form of paternalism.

Rather than attempting to change the rules of the game, the missionary should appropriate the rules so well that they enhance his ministry. He should bend his strategy to fit the culture. George Peters says,

> The ability of Christianity to harness and mobilize the cultural, social and psychological forces of the native environment . . . is of great importance in the evangelization of the masses of people [1970a:199].

THREE COMMON AREAS OF CULTURAL OVERHANG

The creator complex will manifest itself in many different ways, depending upon the culture the particular missionary was born and brought up in. Americans have certain culturally-inbred mental attitudes which often are not recognized as such by missionaries and thus become the hidden cause of retarded church growth. At least three of these are worthy of brief analysis: integration, individualism, and ecclesiastical polity.

1. *The therapeutic drive toward integration.* A deep guilt complex has been building up in the whites of the United States since Africans were first shipped across the Atlantic as slaves. The present racial crisis, a result of reaping what was then sown, has caused a psychological conditioning which is present in almost all American whites, missionaries included. In past generations, mechanisms had been built up which successfully covered over the problem; but in our day black leaders such Malcolm X, Stokely Carmichael, and Rapp Brown have precipitated the long-awaited moment of truth. Centuries of injustice now cannot be denied by the white community. Repentance is commonplace, but just how to make tangible amends for what has been done is the most pressing issue on the conscience of sensitive whites. In a well-intentioned gesture of reconciliation, many whites have stressed the need for integration; and some Christians have made it a virtue equal to intercessory prayer or truthfulness.

Unqualified integration as a goal raises many cultural problems. The old "myth of the melting pot" that most of us learned in grade school drilled into our tender minds the concept that, in spite of the fact Americans came from all over the world, they melted together in one uniform culture once they passed through the immigration office at the port of entry.

This created a staunch refusal on the part of the general public to recognize that black Americans and white Americans are culturally separate even though living in the same nation and saluting the same flag. This anthropological mistake has been at the root of many of today's racial misunderstandings. Creative and lasting solutions to the racial problems will have to be premised on the fact that we are here dealing with a cross-cultural situation, in some respects as pronounced as the difference between whites of the United States and such peoples as the Arabs or the Solomon Islanders.

Black black leaders (as distinguished from *white* black leaders) no more want integration than Mexico wants to become the fifty-first state of the union. What they are asking for is a mature recognition on the part of the whites of the legitimacy of their own cultural values. They want these values to be accepted as equally "American" as those of the white community. They know that the integration of 19 million blacks into a community of almost 200 million whites could mean only one thing: the obliteration of black cultural values. This is why integration is *not* the answer for most blacks. Economic equality, social justice, the abolition of discrimination and prejudice, and proportionate political representation are much more realistic and desired solutions than integration. Black is too beautiful to lose its cultural identity through integration. But this very beauty of the black American culture must be recognized by the white majority both in word and in deed. Laws need to be passed which will preserve black culture, not in integration but in a harmonious and mutually beneficial symbiotic relationship.

This principle needs to be carried over into the church. A local congregation does not do well to force integration in advance of the degree of integration of society as a whole. The attempt of some white churches to enroll a few black families so that the church can be called "integrated" and thus gain certain denominational prestige is scorned by many black blacks as "tokenism." A close investigation of most "integrated" churches in the United States will reveal that the black members are usually those who already have adopted white cultural values to a large extent. In Brazil, on the other hand, intermarriage—the most accurate measure of integration of races—is common and socially accepted (although some pockets of white superiority do exist). There, truly integrated black-white churches are the order of the day, since outside of church the groups share mutual cultural values. In the United States a strong social resistance to black-white marriage is dominant, and therefore integrated churches are neither commonplace nor widely desired by either the black or white community.

Blacks like black churches. They understand the language. They feel more comfortable there. Even in athletics, a field long proud of its "integration," this integration exists largely on the playing field. In a revealing series of articles on the Negro athlete, the *Los Angeles Times* pointed out that off the field, black and white players do not mix so well. When Bernie Casey, Negro flanker of the Los Angeles Rams, was asked to analyze why the players did not sit together in the dining room of the training camp, he said:

> I also have observed segregated seating by choice in dining halls, and I too have thought about it. Why am I sitting at this black table? And I suppose the most straightforward answer I could give myself is that I'm *more comfortable there* [Maher 1968:III:1, itals. added].

Black Christian leaders have begun to make the same type of statements. Whereas they once thought that the only pathway open to them was to imitate whites as much as they could, the liberation movement now has allowed blacks to swing back to more culturally relevant patterns. As *TIME* commented:

> In the pursuit of "relevancy," Negro churches in the North have been returning to the soulful spirit of the past in worship—and becoming more militant in political concern. Many congregations that had tried to imitate the sobriety of their white counterparts are again beginning to emphasize zeal and fervor in both sermon and song [1968:70].

William Willoughby reinforces this by commenting that "the liturgy of most white churches would continue to hold little appeal for the black who is not bent on 'whitening' his native cultural tendencies" (1969:44). As blacks become more and more liberated, they probably will desire fewer integrated churches on the congregational level. One pronounced trend will no doubt be toward making black churches blacker, even though some black churches may become whiter.

A principle can be extracted from all this which should be generally applied to the matter of ecclesiastical integration. The *local congregation* may well choose to be only as integrated as the families it serves. If blacks and whites intermarry freely and live in harmonious family relationships, the integrated congregation will be the most meaningful for their church life; and they will want to make it their church home. But if intermarriage is not yet practiced, if it is the exception rather than the rule, all concerned may feel more comfortable in churches in which they are free to reflect their cultural values. The Reverend L. T. Rice of Washington's Corinth Baptist Church says that in his area 30-40 percent of the black storefront churches have a Pentecostal-Holiness type of liturgy, which, in contrast, runs only 3-4 percent among American Christians in general.

We have a different situation on the *denominational* level, however. The denomination should not reflect only the family structure, as does the congregation, but rather the broader aspects of society. In a country where integration is accepted in sports, schools, employment, and entertainment, denominational integration is meaningful. In Christ, black congregations and white congregations should be able to work together in harmony and to their mutual benefit, as long as equal rights are preserved and as long as the minority churches do not get the idea that they are joining a denomination which imposes majority cultural values.

This situation involving blacks and whites relates basically to the United States, but the principles apply equally to missionary churches. The misguided idea that promoting unqualified integration is good therapy for the American racial guilt complex can cause unwarranted trouble in missionary churches, especially where a multicultural situation prevails. J. H. Bavinck admits that "from a purely theological point of view it seems as if we ought to press for the formation of a single church," but then adds,

However, in this broken world there are other reasons that may make it undesirable to seek to unite heterogeneous elements into a single church. There are factors that make such a congregation extremely difficult, yes, even impracticable. . . . A Chinese feels more at home in a church which not only preaches in his own language but also in figures and illustrations which apply to him [1964:166-167].

Forced and unnatural integration often has been the cause of stunted church growth. People like to become Christians in comfortable surroundings. They like the freedom to express their own cultural values in church without worrying that they might offend others, knowing that these expressions will be understood and accepted.

Some who oppose this point of view seek support in Galatians 3:28, which says, "there is neither Jew nor Greek, there is neither bond nor free, there is neither male nor female; for ye are all one in Christ Jesus." Only superficial exegesis could understand this as a proof text for what we have been calling unqualified integration. The context in Galatians 3 is not an exposition of the unity of the church (as are 1 Corinthians 12 and Ephesians 4, for example). Paul here is dealing with the matter of how a *Gentile* can become a Christian. In context, all this verse says is that, in order for a Gentile to become a Christian, he does not have to become a Jew first, as some of the Galatians thought. A slave does not have to become free before he can be a Christian, nor does a woman have to become a man. Instead of teaching integration, Paul is saying that a Gentile does *not* have to become culturally integrated into the Jewish community in order to be accepted into the body of Christ. The church has room for legitimate Jews and legitimate Gentiles. A believer can remain culturally a Greek, socially a slave, sexually a woman, and still be a good Christian.

2. *The insistence on free enterprise.* One of the most natural cultural overhangs from an individualistic society like the United States is the insistence on free enterprise. From the days of the six-gun law on the frontier, the people of the United States have developed an individualistic, egocentric, dog-eat-dog cultural pattern. Most Americans today place a high value

on "doing your own thing" and "getting ahead." Survival of the fittest has been the backbone of our economic system; and since it has been relatively successful, we have come to the point of identifying capitalism with the will of God.

When Americans arrive in a second culture, they often carry along with them this insistence on individuality. In shopping, they have a hard time understanding why merchants don't cut prices and sell more volume. In evangelism, they press for individual decisions but shy away from anything that looks like a mass decision—or, in McGavran's refined terminology, a multiindividual people movement.

Whereas it is true that in the final analysis individuals, not groups, decide for Christ, it is equally true that in many societies individuals have been culturally programmed not to make an individual decision without first checking with the group. This might seem strange to an American who has been programmed to "do his thing." This would horrify a man from a group-oriented culture. He could think of doing nothing but "the group's thing." If the presentation of the gospel is not adapted to this cultural characteristic, the kingdom of God is retarded. George Peters expresses it well when he says,

> There is an ethnic, or group, or people approach in evangelism which has been either overlooked or ignored by the Westerner, not because it is not in the Bible, but because of his mentality of individualism [1970a:173-174].

3. *Ecclesiastical polity.* Cultural overhang in the area of ecclesiastical polity has been commented upon a great deal in recent literature. There is no doubt that lack of sensitivity in this area has hindered both qualitative and quantitative growth of churches in the Third World. Where churches have been free to develop along culturally meaningful lines, such as in the Chilean Pentecostal churches, healthy growth has usually resulted.

It is more difficult to distinguish between what the Bible actually prescribes and what is culturally-conditioned in church matters than in other areas. Since we have always done a thing in a certain way in our American churches, we feel that we have had divine approval. Perhaps it is true that God has approved certain practices in our particular culture, but at the same time we must be open to divine approval of quite distinct patterns in other cultures.

The manifestations of this phenomenon are so numerous that a separate chapter could be written on them. But many of them are obvious, and further elaboration would be tedious. Let us just conclude with a list of a few of the aspects of church life which might well be reexamined in the light of what we have been saying about cultural overhang.

1. The need for professional pastors
2. The necessity that a pastor be full-time, with salary paid by his church
3. The need for specially constructed church buildings
4. Sunday schools as essential for Christian education
5. Certain days and hours for church services
6. Exaggerated educational standards for the ministry
7. Universal validity of specific liturgical forms
8. Superiority of democratic church government
9. Absolutizing certain musical values, such as four-part harmony
10. Transposing culturally determined ethical standards: degrees of dress or undress, truthfulness and promise-keeping, punctuality, cleanliness
11. Requiring certain standards of doctrinal orthodoxy on the basis of culturally and historically conditioned creeds

6

Anticipatory Strategy

MISSIONARY STRATEGY deals with the future. It attempts to answer the question, How can we best use the resources that God has given us in the days ahead? To a large extent, then, missionary strategy must be based on predictions or at least on some intelligent anticipation of the future. This makes it necessary for us to address ourselves to the preliminary question of whether predictions should be made at all in Christian work. After that, we will be able to move on to the matter of how predictions for missionary strategy should be made.

ARE PREDICTIONS LEGITIMATE IN CHRISTIAN WORK?

Many Christians have reacted against a church-growth-oriented theology, claiming that it amounts to a substitution of human means for the working of the Holy Spirit. It is unfortunate that this impression has been created, because such a desire is far removed from the intentions of the leaders of the church growth movement. Some of the spiritually oriented objections that have been raised are as follows:

1. "God . . . giveth the increase" (1 Co 3:7) and "the wind bloweth where it listeth" (John 3:8). Man is not to know from where the wind comes nor where it goes. Only God knows whether a given church will grow or whether it will not. Man has no right to dictate to the Holy Spirit. "We don't know the future, but we do know the One who holds the future in His hands."

2. "Not by might, nor by power, but by my Spirit, saith the LORD" (Zec 4:6). The attempt to predict the growth or nongrowth of churches substitutes man-made schemes for God's power. God wishes to manifest His own power to the nations.

Human calculations and technological gimmicks used to declare where God will work or where He will not work usurp the glory from God.

3. Regeneration is the sovereign work of the Holy Spirit in the heart of a sinner. In no sense can it be considered the result of a predictable interplay of cultural, anthropological, psychological, and sociological factors.

4. James says, "ye know not what shall be on the next day. . . . For ye ought to say, If the Lord will, we shall live, and do this, or that" (4:14-15). Any Christian who does not obey this is presumptuous.

These arguments are not without weight. They serve a good purpose in pointing up the dangers of doing the Lord's work in ways not approved by the Lord. It is quite possible for God's servants to become haughty and insensitive to the leading of the Holy Spirit. Original sin makes us all susceptible to the temptation of taking the glory from God and ascribing it to ourselves. But this everpresent danger should not cause us to overreact and be blind to spiritually oriented reasons why missionary leaders *should* predict church growth as one of the bases for sound strategy planning.

1. Rather than leaving the Holy Spirit to one side, intelligent predictions as to the growth of the church are made out of obedience to God. One looks to the Holy Spirit for His wisdom and guidance *before* mistakes are made or resources squandered. Spiritual guidance in an anticipatory dimension is not foreign to Christian work, as any preacher who prepares sermons beforehand will testify. Experience of godly men has shown that looking to the Spirit for His guidance before entering the pulpit is not presumptuous but rather good homiletical procedure, resulting in improved messages. By the same token, taking an aspirin for a headache does not necessarily imply that the patient does not believe that God could have healed him without a humanly-manufactured aspirin pill. But most devoted Christian men agree that in the fields of homiletics and medicine the Lord expects us to use whatever means we have at our disposal, in conjunction with our constant dependence on Him. It is a curious phenomenon that some would exclude evangelistic and missionary work from this same principle.

Psalm 32 contains that magnificent verse concerning the guidance of the Lord: "I will instruct thee and teach thee in the way which thou shalt go; I will guide thee with mine eye" (v. 8). While this verse is frequently quoted, the implications of the very next verse are seldom brought out. It warns, "Be ye not as the horse, or as the mule, which have no understanding." Horses and mules were not created in the image of God, and therefore they have no understanding. Human beings have this and should use it. As God guides us, He expects us to be like intelligent adults, not stupid animals. If our hearts are tender toward Him, we can use our full powers of reason; and He will faithfully guide us by them and give us understanding above our own when we need it. Carnal intelligence, the *sophia* of the Corinthians, is not good. But the wisdom of God, the *theo sophian* (1 Co 1:24) is a gift from God that He expects us to use.

2. The process of predicting church growth is another term for simply testing the soils to determine which is the most fertile and which is relatively barren. As we have seen, the law of sowing tells us that time and resources are not wisely spent on sowing the seed in soil which obviously will never produce fruit. God is not pleased with inefficient sowers. They are poor stewards of God's resources. Wherever these resources can be put to the use that will bring more men and women to faith in Christ, this pleases Him. In order to help us do this, God has given us certain indications so that we can discern where the fertile soil really is.

3. The alternative to predicting church growth or testing the soil would be to ask God to give some supernatural word whenever He wants a specific task done. A celestial printout delivered at eight o'clock each morning would be a wonderful thing for Christian workers. But evidently God has no more chosen to work in that manner than He has chosen to cure simple headaches without aspirin. Paul's Macedonian vision was an example of what God can do, but it is not a norm. We should strive to avoid the mistake of the Sadducees:

> When it is evening, ye say, It will be fair weather; for the sky is red. And in the morning, It will be foul weather today; for the sky is red and overcast. O ye hypocrites, ye can discern

the face of the sky; but can ye not discern the signs of the times? [Mt. 16:2-3].

The Sadducees were seeking some spectacular manifestation, like a celestial printout; and Jesus had to reprimand them because they refused to see the hand of God working in the ordinary development of history around them. An objective look at much missionary work today might reveal the same thing.

4. Only the Holy Spirit can do the work of regeneration. As far as I am informed, no evangelical is debating this point. But for some reason known only to God, He has chosen to use human beings to accomplish His purposes in salvation, short of the act of regeneration. The process is spelled out in Romans 10: "Faith cometh by hearing" (v. 17) and "how shall they hear without a preacher?" (v. 14). Regeneration remains a mystery, but communication of the gospel to those whom the Holy Spirit will regenerate is not. Although it is a terrifying thought, it is true that if God's servants do not evangelize, evangelism will not take place.

God, therefore, expects His servants to evangelize; and He desires that they evangelize well. This implies making the most sacrificial, intelligent, efficient, and dedicated effort to be sure that every bit of the whitened harvest is reaped. Anticipatory strategy, or predicting church growth, is one of the best means God has given us to accomplish His will in world evangelism.

5. An illustration of this can be seen in the parable of the ten virgins (Mt 25:1-13). Although the thrust of the parable is to awaken the hearers to the need for living in constant expectancy of the Lord's return, in the story itself one of the differences between the wise and foolish virgins was precisely in the area of anticipatory strategy. All predicted when the bridegroom would arrive. The foolish ones, through whatever data they might have had, came to the erroneous conclusion that he would come early. The wise ones had arrived at the correct prediction that he might come later, so they took extra oil. Good anticipatory strategy got them into the wedding hall and made them pleasing to their master.

6. Finally, it must be recognized that even the best methods known to predict church growth *are* human. None of them can

be classified as divine. As human methods, they have limitations and are fallible. They must be used with caution. All anticipatory strategy, therefore, must be considered as tentative; and the worker must be alert to other factors which God might bring in to change the situation at any time.

How Church Growth Can Be Anticipated

It is one thing to establish the fact that anticipatory strategy in missionary work is desirable, but quite another to ask whether it is possible to predict church growth. This type of procedure has not played a very prominent part in missionary planning up to now, which accounts in part for the negative reaction that some have developed against it. Since few have tried it, some still question that it is even within the realm of possibility.

Since 1960, when the Institute of Church Growth was founded by Donald McGavran, hundreds of missionary associates have worked with professors of missions there to develop instruments for making predictions as to where churches would be likely to grow and where they would be likely not to grow. The decade of effort has borne some fruit, and the next decade of accelerated research and experimentation is likely to produce proportionately more. The science of church growth is still a young one, and a relative newcomer to missiology. Therefore, the possibilities for anticipatory strategy are still limited; but some of the more promising ones can be described at least in a general way.

THE GROWTH RATE OF OTHER CHURCHES

Wherever some churches are actually growing among a certain people, others probably can grow there also. Presently we are witnessing an extraordinary growth of churches on the continent of Africa, for example. According to David Barrett, Christianity in Africa south of the Sahara is increasing from 3 percent of the population in 1900 to 46 percent in 2000. In Latin America the Protestant church is growing three times the rate of the population in general. Great ingatherings have been reported in Indonesia, and among hippie-types on the West Coast of the United States. Growth in these places is likely to continue in the near future for any denomination geared toward reaping the whitened harvest.

In order to visualize past and present growth rates, graphs should be drawn for all possible churches. Plotting these on logarithmic paper will show not only absolute membership growth but also the variations in rate. At a glance one can see where the rate of growth is increasing, holding its own, or decreasing. Where churches are growing at healthy rates, investment of further resources in ways which will enhance further growth is wise. Where rates are falling off, more caution should be exercised unless methods definitely can be improved.

Statistics for a whole continent are not useful for strategy planning, except to furnish general clues. Even national statistics will be too vague to be helpful. The most meaningful statistics will enable the leader to plot the growth of the churches within specific ethnic groupings and in specific geographic locations. This is the reason why denominational statistics, especially in heterogeneous denominations, are not always useful.

While there is need for anticipatory strategy for the planting of new churches, it is needed also to maintain good health in already growing churches. Quentin Nordyke, for example, recently took inventory of the Friends Church in Bolivia and projected that at the present rate of growth, it would not be improbable for the church to increase from 7,000 members in 1970 to 220,000 in 1990. There is no theological reason to doubt that it would be God's will for His church to multiply that rapidly. The penetrating question then becomes Will the missionaries and national leaders be so prepared for the rapid growth of the church that they will not become unwitting *obstacles* to the work of the Holy Spirit? Nordyke suggests that a combination of the proper psychological attitudes toward rapid growth, expanded plans for leadership training through extension, theological education, and the utilization of every possible technological aid will be necessary if healthy growth is not to be retarded.

Nongrowth is just as important to discover as growth. If no churches are growing in a given area, anticipatory strategy might lead to another more promising area. In some sections of Los Angeles, for example, the Spanish-American population is moving in and taking over from the Anglos. The Anglo churches are static, and therefore these zones are not good places to plant new Anglo churches.

SOCIAL AND ECONOMIC CHANGE

Wherever people are undergoing rapid or radical social and economic change, churches are likely to grow. People who are uprooted from familiar social surroundings and located in new ones find themselves searching for a new orientation to their lives. They are disposed to listen to the gospel, and many of them will recognize that Christ can become the integrating factor they need in their personal lives and in their community.

Areas of rapid urbanization almost invariably contain large segments of population receptive to the gospel. In Hong Kong many people are turning to Christ. In open high-rise apartments, evangelism is fruitful. On the other hand, closed-community high-rises with doormen and microphones over the doorbells have not proven receptive.

Where new industry has changed the economic pattern of an area or where new roads are opening profitable markets for agricultural goods, churches are likely to grow.

Colonization and relocation projects which move peasants from one part of the country to another usually will be fruitful fields, especially if the colonists are forging a new society. On the other hand, entire ethnic units which migrate to a new area for colonization but which retain their traditional language and customs will not usually be fruitful unless reached by evangelists from their own culture.

A study of the Italian immigrants to Brazil, for example, reveals some of these principles in action. As Read, Monterroso, and Johnson point out (1969:214), the Italian immigrants to Brazil around the turn of the century were a fertile field for the gospel. But the gospel did not come to them through Portuguese-speaking Brazilians. It was preached by Louis Francescon, an Italian-American from the United States who preached in Italian. Today the churches resulting from his ministry include over 500,000 members. Here was a combination of a ripe field and proper methods.

But the important fact is that not all the Italian immigrants in Brazil wanted to become Christians. There were two kinds: the winegrowers from northern Italy and the factory workers from southern Italy and Sicily. The northern Italians formed new communities in Brazil which reproduced their old Italian way of life. They were not receptive to the gospel. On the other hand, the southern Italians, caught up with Brazilian urbanization and industrialization, had broken with their old way of life and had become receptive.

When similar situations come about in other parts of the world, church-growth men will tend to project possibilities of growth and nongrowth on the basis of data on past experience. Therefore, those who change their life style most radically will be the ones approached first with the gospel, since it is likely that solid, growing churches can be planted among them. Those who cling to their former ways will come lower on the priority scale.

Among animistic peoples where westernization is inexorably sweeping in, large masses of receptive people can be found. They definitely are going to leave their animism and adopt new spiritual values. If the gospel of Christ is preached to them, many will embrace it gladly. Alan Tippett estimates that something around 200 million people will leave animism in this generation. Will they become Christians?

This type of people present a whitened harvest field but is not necessarily one that remains ripe for a long period of time. The best estimates calculate that people involved in rapid social change will remain receptive to the gospel in their new surroundings for up to five years. After that, the receptivity curve slopes off considerably; because, if they have not found Christ by then, they very likely have found a substitute and have lost their interest in hearing the gospel.

POLITICAL CHANGES

News of political change and its implications, such as this report from Bishop Chandu Ray of Singapore, excites churchmen who are properly tuned in to anticipatory strategy:

> Conservative Islam was defeated at the polls in East Pakistan when the Awami league won 98% of the vote. What Islam

lost at the polls, the military dictatorship is trying to restore. Conservative Muslim leaders are being quoted in Pakistani press all the time. They, of course, uphold the military regime in the name of Islam. There are some indications that a widespread disillusionment with Islam itself has set in [1971c:3].

Such political changes frequently have caused people to become responsive. The harvest in Bangladesh may be ripening. World War II made the Japanese responsive for a time, and many of them were won for Christ. The war refugees in South Vietnam now are considered a fertile field. Such situations, however, are usually only temporary; and the opportunities must be bought up quickly.

Revolution and counterrevolution will often produce receptivity. A revolutionary country can be expected to be more open to change and new ideas than a reactionary one, other things being equal. The mountain peasants of Bolivia, for example, have been more receptive than their cousins in Peru, a phenomenon which can be traced to the Bolivian social revolution of 1952. Now that Peru has become a revolutionary country also, it would be reasonable to predict that Peruvian peasants will be much more responsive, especially when land reform becomes effective and they are freed from the oppression of the feudal landlords.

During the first few years of Evangelism in Depth in Latin America, observers noted that, when a revolution was somehow fortuitously associated with the campaign, the results seemed better than in countries where no political problems presented themselves. In the Dominican Republic, where American troops invaded, and in Guatemala, where the President attended the final EID service with a loaded machine gun in his hands, results were more satisfactory than in peaceful Costa Rica.

When a people are oppressed for an extended period of time and do not enjoy liberty of thought and action, they often become highly receptive to the gospel when the oppression is finally removed. Some believe that Mainland China for that very reason is the greatest potential mission field in the world today. When the ideological oppression lifts, multitudes of

Chinese undoubtedly will choose Christ over Mao if they hear the gospel in relevant terms.

SYSTEMS ANALYSIS AND ELECTRONIC DATA PROCESSING

Up to now, the process of gathering enough data so that church growth could be more accurately predicted has been very difficult. Observation, experience, and educated guesswork were the chief tools. Many of these guesses were very good ones, however, and infinitely superior to no anticipatory strategy at all.

But now that the technological world has made electronic data processing systems (EDP) available to missions, new and sophisticated possibilities have opened up. This is still a pioneer mission field in the true sense of the word. The fact that pith helmets, machetes, and Anopheles mosquitos have been replaced by neckties, keyboards, and air-conditioning does not reduce the pioneering aspect of the task. World Vision has assigned to its MARC (Missions Advanced Research and Communication) division the task of pioneering the use of computer technology in the field of missionary strategy.

MARC is beginning with Brazil. With such competent staff members as William Read (author of *New Patterns of Church Growth in Brazil*) and Frank Ineson (former executive secretary of the Brazilian Missionary Information Bureau), they are moving ahead with the task of programming masses of data into the computers so that meaningful information eventually will be forthcoming. Their first interpretative bulletin, *Continuing Evangelism in Brazil*, was published in January 1971.

It is hoped that they soon will be able to make predictions based on hard statistical data for the following questions.

Where is the church most likely to grow? Which countries have the greatest potential, and which particular groups of people within those countries show signs of being receptive to the gospel? In other words, by careful soil tests, missionary strategists should be able to advise the sowers where they should plant the seed first.

Who are the people most likely to become faithful Christians? The MARC project has seemed thus far to indicate that

in Brazil factory workers and their families are the most likely
to become Christians. This was discovered by plotting the
density of the evangelical population on a map and then super-
imposing another map showing the density of industrial activity. William Read says, "It hits you in the face!" One conclusion from this recent discovery is that, as long as a significant portion of Brazilian factory workers have not yet come to
Christ, here is a whitened field, an area which should receive
the highest evangelistic priority.

When is the time to move in? The harvesters must move in
when the fruit is ripe, not while it is still green nor after it has
rotted. To take an obvious example, now is not yet the time
to move into Mainland China, at least for American missionaries. The fruit is still green. On the other hand, in indus-
trialized Japan the whitened harvest of the forties and fifties has
largely passed.

What resources are needed for an efficient job? Specific missionaries are needed for specific tasks. If the university student
community in a socialist country turns ripe, one type of worker
will be needed. If a group of animistic peasants turns ripe,
someone with different qualifications is needed. Part of good
management is to look ahead and, as much as possible, determine where the needs will be and what kind of missionary
should be recruited or reassigned.

As Parkinson's "law" (that work expands to fill the time
allotted) well illustrates, the progress toward established goals
is not always directly proportionate to the number of workers
involved. Any staff can easily reach a point of diminishing returns, a danger for missionaries as much as for the aerospace
industry.

Some material resources are usually needed to get the job
done properly. This phase of the operation should be carefully
planned, however. If an automobile or a duplicator or a video
tape recorder is needed, provision should be made for it ahead
of time. On the other hand, senseless multiplying of gadgets
(a frequent occurrence on the mission field) should be avoided.

How should strategy be planned? Methods and approaches
should be used which will most likely result in people hearing
and understanding the gospel, committing their lives to Christ,

and establishing churches. No method in itself should be taken for granted. In his incisive analysis of one of the current popular evangelistic movements, Malcolm Bradshaw says that "it is doubtful whether uniformed activism will produce much growth" (1969:114). He suggests that leaders of this particular movement undertake careful precampaign research to "ascertain the actual shape of the churches and missions in the campaign." "As such data is compiled," Bradshaw continues, "there will emerge a culturally appropriate strategy of action, indicated by the needs and resources of the area" (1969:115, 116). Bradshaw is advocating anticipatory strategy.

EXAMPLES OF A NEED FOR ANTICIPATORY STRATEGY

Good examples to illustrate the need for anticipatory strategy abound in the scores of scholarly studies on church growth which have been done in recent years. A need now exists for some writer to extract fifteen or twenty of them and make them available to a wider public. This would be a significant tool for missionary strategists in the future. At this point we will present only three brief case studies.

SAN JOSE DE SISA, PERU

Data for this case study was furnished by Stewart McIntosh of the Regions Beyond Missionary Union. He relates how San José de Sisa, a small town in the jungle area of northern Peru, has been an RBMU "mission station" from the early days of the work. For twenty years the mission had assigned one or two missionary women to the station for "missionary work."

The town was typical of the area in that it contained two kinds of people: Spanish-speaking mestizos and lower-class Quechuas. The mestizos controlled the commerce, the transportation, and the government of the town. The Quechuas were the agricultural and laboring class. Most of the Quechua men could handle Spanish, but Quechua was the language of the home and the heart.

The missionaries set their goal at "reaching" the mestizo class, on the theory that when the higher class is won to Christ, the lower class will follow. After twenty years, only six converts had been made. Was San José de Sisa a barren fig tree that needed to be chopped down? This would have been a reasonable conclusion. But the problem lay rather in the area of anticipatory strategy. The "mestizo first" theory was poor church-growth planning, as subsequent events proved.

In 1960 a Bible school dropout, Victor Cenepo, was sent to San José de Sisa because at the time there were no missionaries to send. He was small in stature, slightly crippled, and not an eloquent speaker (a description curiously similar to some of the apostle Paul). Cenepo was not able to continue the former mission strategy in San José, because the mestizos wouldn't listen to him at all—he was a Quechua. Through necessity, he turned from the mestizos to the Quechuas and preached his first sermon in the Quechua tongue, telling the story of Noah's ark. Four from one family decided for Christ that night. For several successive nights they brought more of their own extended family, and soon the entire family was Christian. By 1968 one third of the village had been evangelized and were in the evangelical church. One hundred had been baptized as church members, and two hundred fifty attended Sunday school. In the process several mestizos, more than during the previous twenty years, had given their hearts to Christ. The church outgrew the new building by 1971.

For twenty years the responsive Quechuas had not been reached by the gospel. A whole generation passed into eternity without repentance and faith. The missionaries are not to be blamed; they worked to the best of their knowledge and abilities. They did not have the instruments for anticipatory strategy that we have today. This story is told not to criticize the past but rather to sound a warning for the present, wherever missionaries may be laboring in seemingly unfruitful fields when right nearby an unobserved whitened harvest awaits the reapers.

SEVENTH DAY ADVENTISTS IN BOLIVIA

Some of the marginal denominations and false cults have been using principles of anticipatory strategy for a long time, to their decided advantage. Perhaps the Seventh Day Adventist missionaries to Bolivia could not have articulated the principles of this section, but they applied them nonetheless.

As of 1930, five missions had solidly established missionary work in Bolivia. Of the five, the Adventists were the youngest. Yet, their membership exceeded the *combined* membership of the other four. What was the reason? Not sheepstealing, as they frequently have been accused, for they were working in a separate area from the rest. Hopefully, it was not a more biblical message. No, the key is that they were working among a receptive people—the Aymara Indians. The other missions were working among mestizos in the cities and Quechuas in the country with relatively scant results.

Again, the other four missions did not have the tools that today's missionaries have. They were not aware of the Adventist growth; and, even if they had been, it is doubtful whether this would have affected their mission policies. In those days mission decisions were not based on what we have been calling anticipatory strategy—activity was largely based on "need." Better missionary strategy in those years might have searched for and found thousands of Aymara lost sheep and brought them into the fold before it was too late.

UNITED STATES DENOMINATION XYZ

A certain denomination in the United States, which we will simply call XYZ, is facing a problem in strategy planning not uncommon among city churches in many parts of the country. It is traditionally a white, middle-class denomination of moderate size, confined to one state. Here is the recent history of three of its churches.

Church 1 was an inner-city church, one of the denomination's oldest. Its neighborhood became Spanish-American; but the church continued to be white, middle-class, with more and more of its members commuting to the meetings from outlying communities. The young people began falling away, and the average age of the congregation kept rising. Membership began to shrink. Very few were won from the immediate neighborhood, since the average Spanish-American was not interested in worshiping with Anglos and hearing English sermons. The church was finally closed, and the building sold to a Spanish-speaking congregation of another denomination.

Church 2 is in one of the older suburbs. For some time the

membership has peaked, but the church is holding its own. The older church members have remained in the community, but their children are purchasing less-expensive housing in the newer suburbs and joining churches nearer their homes. Spanish-speaking families are moving in rapidly, and the ratio of Spanish-Americans to Anglos is increasing. The church wonders what to do.

Church 3 was planted in a new suburb as a daughter church of Number 2 and other XYZ churches at the time the land was being bulldozed for new housing. It has developed with the community and now is growing so fast that three Sunday morning services are needed to accommodate all the worshipers. It has been instrumental in planting another rapidly growing church in a still newer suburb.

If anticipatory strategy was not used in the case of Church 1, it should now be used for Church 2. This church should not allow itself to become sealed off from the growing Spanish-American population, so that someday it will find itself with little opportunity for ministry in the community. Two alternatives are open to the denomination. Either it should decide to become bicultural and make a definite effort to plant culturally relevant churches among the Spanish-Americans, or it should decide to remain monocultural and concentrate on planting churches in the newer suburbs and let other denominations minister to the Spanish-Americans. If XYZ does not do either of these (or a combination of both), the future holds little hope for growth in that area.

THE RESISTANT AREAS

Upon hearing for the first time about planning missionary strategy according to anticipated results in terms of new disciples rather than according to that nebulous concept of "need," many naturally become concerned about the work among resistant peoples. This is a legitimate concern, and much more study should be done on resistant peoples and potential church growth among them. But some conclusions are fairly evident.

The Muslims, for example, are considered one of the most resistant peoples. Should we bypass them? Of course not. We should pay as much attention to the Muslims in our strategy planning as we do to the Taiwanese, the Nicaraguans, or the Zen Buddhists. Not all Muslims are resistant to the gospel. Several hundred thousand of them recently have come to Christ in Indonesia, and more seem ready to do so. Some groups of Muslims in Ethiopia now are trusting the risen Lord as their Saviour. Just as other peoples, some Muslims resist the message and some accept it. Good anticipatory strategy will test the soil among Muslims before beginning to sow the seed. Soil-testing missionaries are urgently needed to tell evangelists where the most likely place for the seed sowing is. The report from Bangladesh by Chandu Ray, quoted earlier in this chapter, is a good example of this. Bangladesh demands very close watching and accurate soil testing in the years ahead. When the soil among the Muslims there, or in any other place, becomes fertile, the sowers should move in to do the job and then reap the harvest.

The conclusion that a people is resistant to the gospel should not be reached hastily. Other deeper investigations should be made. Perhaps the cultural approach is wrong, as it was in the case of San José de Sisa. The people there were thought to be resistant to the gospel, but the problem was that the approach was not directed toward those who in fact were receptive. Again, the methods may be wrong. If you are using tract distribution to attempt to evangelize a semiliterate people, you may well conclude that they are resistant. But with the same people, a home-evangelism method may prove to be very fruitful.

7

Evangelism and Saturation Evangelism

ONE OF THE MOST FREQUENTLY HEARD expressions in missionary circles today is *saturation evangelism*. We do well, then, to make an effort to understand what saturation evangelism means and how the concept fits into contemporary missionary strategy. Before doing that, however, we should wrestle with the definition of evangelism itself.

THE EVANGELISTIC RENEWAL OF THE 1960s

One recent observer called the decade of the sixties "the winter of the church." In many respects it did seem as if the gates of hell were rising up to abolish what God had wrought. Theology became secularized in many quarters, situation ethics threatened to guide the behavior of Christians, pessimism followed in the wake of the retreat of the colonial West, neo-universalism surfaced in pulpits, the Vietnam war convulsed the world, the Kennedy brothers and Martin Luther King were assassinated, a death-of-God theology emerged from dying churches, the hippie movement manifested open social rebellion, youth revolt and campus uprisings were commonplace, ghettos were burned mercilessly, police brutality followed as a reaction, church attendance plummeted, and many denominations cut back drastically on their missionary programs.

At the same time the decade of the sixties saw amazing growth of the Christian church, especially below the thirtieth parallel. World alignments shifted in such a way that in a sense it became more meaningful to talk of North-South rather than East-West. As the decade ended, out of the winter of the church God had brought forth some green sprouts which presaged a new springtime in the seventies.

Among these green sprouts was the revival of worldwide interest in evangelism on a massive scale. In order to accomplish this, God used three extraordinary men. They were extraordinary, not only because of their gifts but also because each of them was creative enough to build a means of perpetuating his own ministry and thus multiply his influence on the church. The unique combination of three men and three events contributed to a new mood of evangelism in the Christian church. Who were the men and what were the events?

Donald A. McGavran is the father of the church-growth theology which has become so influential in all aspects of current missiology. His event was the launching of the *Institute of Church Growth* as a graduate department of Northwest Christian College in Eugene, Oregon, in 1960. Under the providence of God, it was transferred to Fuller Theological Seminary in 1965 and has remained in Pasadena as the School of World Mission and Institute of Church Growth. This school has become a respected center of missionary research and writing, and church growth theology has spurred many to renewed efforts in evangelism and missions.

R. Kenneth Strachan, as general director of the Latin America Mission, developed what was to become the prototype of saturation evangelism movements—the concept of "evangelism in depth." The symbolic event was the first *Evangelism in Depth* campaign, held in Nicaragua in 1961. Even after Strachan's untimely death in middecade, saturation evangelism has continued to gain momentum not only in Latin America but also in other parts of the world.

Billy Graham, who now has become an evangelist celebrity, could just as easily have done his own thing and passed on to his reward as many powerful evangelists before him have done. But Graham did something more than just that. The event that will perpetuate his ministry and influence was the *World Congress on Evangelism* held in Berlin in 1966. Subsequent congresses on evangelism which have eminated from Berlin have influenced churchmen in every continent and virtually every country for new and creative participation in evangelism.

McGavran, Strachan, and Graham were God's principal instruments for bringing about a new mood of evangelism throughout the church of Christ. They were not all; many others could be added to the list. God is turning field after field ripe unto the harvest, and He is preparing the reapers for what may be the greatest ingathering that church history has seen yet.

DEFINING EVANGELISM

Every book on missions and evangelism should come to grips sooner or later with a precise definition of evangelism. Curiously, however, not one book in five does it. In many cases, those who write on evangelism assume the word is so commonly understood that it needs no definition. Even when an effort is made to define it, the result is often foggy and confusing.

For example, some have a tendency to define evangelism as whatever they might be doing at the time. This means that the world could describe such disparate activities as radio broadcasting, building roads, school teaching, leading a choir, translating the Bible, teaching English to university students, holding citywide campaigns, printing tracts, or explaining the four spiritual laws. Are all these things really evangelism?

One of the finest scholarly studies on the subject in recent times is Michael Green's book, *Evangelism in the Early Church.* In it, Green makes a thorough study of the three key biblical words related to evangelism: *euaggelizesthai* (to tell the good news), *kerussein* (to proclaim), and *marturein* (to bear witness) (1970:48). He shows how each of these three concepts adds an important dimension to the proclamation of the early church. He also is one of those who gives a crisp definition of evangelism:

> Evangelism in the strict sense is proclaiming the good news of salvation to men and women with a view to their conversion to Christ and incorporation in his church [1970:7].

This definition gives us an excellent starting point for this section. But in order to clarify it even more, we need to contrast it with some of the alternative contemporary definitions.

The definitions given by modern-day writers on evangelism tend to fall into one of three general classifications. For the sake of clarity, I have found the terms *presence, proclamation,* and *persuasion* very helpful as titles for these categories. Green's definition, for example, would be in the persuasion category.

PRESENCE VERSUS PROCLAMATION

"Christian presence" has been a recurring theme in much missiological writing during the past decade. Such names as Charles de Foucald, a French Jesuit missionary, and Jacques Ellul, another Frenchman, are commonly cited as sources for this terminology and concept. Colin Williams calls Christian presence a "code word" (1966:12), because it is used so often today. Max Warren is editor of a whole series of books called Christian Presence Series. The World Student Christian Federation in 1965 gave wide publicity to the idea through its publication, *Student World*. Particularly in conciliar circles, Christian presence came to be considered by many as "the basic form of witness" (Orchard 1964:92).

The influential WSCF report (1965) contended that the words *evangelization, witness,* and *mission* were no longer communicating to students. Students rightly had become concerned about an image they had received of a high-pressure, personality-destroying type of evangelism which insisted on speaking before it listened. It appeared to some that the word *evangelism* was simply a pious cover-up for spiritual brainwashing.

This concern that evangelistic methods not be abused should be a concern for all, not just for WSCF members. In order properly to communicate the gospel, the evangelist must take whatever steps are necessary to identify with his hearers, to know their culture and their problems, to love them as fellow human beings, and to explain the gospel in a way that will be relevant to them. In order to accomplish this, Christian presence, in the sense of physical, cultural, and human involvement, is a sine qua non for evangelism. If this were all that was meant by *Christian presence* we would not even have brought it up as a subject of debate.

But there is much more involved than that. The WSCF report reflects a definite aversion to "a certainty of faith and purpose, an ability to conceptualize faith." It questions whether the Christian faith *can* be communicated with words. The concept of a silent and anonymous evangelist emerges: "Once we are there, we may witness fearlessly to Christ, if the occasion is given; *we may have to be silent.*" This reflects some deep theological presuppositions in the area of the objective of Christian missions; and at this point of objectives, goals, or ends the debate is carried on.

For Christian presence people, the concept of making disciples as the goal of missions is not a frequently played theme. The primary objective of the Christian church in the world is not defined as bringing multitudes to faith in Jesus as Lord and obedience to Him. People should rather recognize Jesus for what He is and stay where they are, involved in the fierce fight against all that dehumanizes, ready to act against demonic powers, to identify with the outcast. Christian mission thus becomes another form of social involvement rather than a conscious attempt, through Christian presence, to proclaim the gospel to every creature and persuade people to become Christians. The stated objective is more frequently to restore normal manhood as we see it in Jesus rather than to baptize them in the name of the Father, and the Son, and the Holy Spirit.

Whatever good work the church does, becomes evangelism, according to this definition. Harvey Cox says, for example, "Any distinction between social action and evangelism is a mistaken one" (quoted in Fiske 1966). Colin Williams agrees that "the distinction between individual evangelism and evangelism calling for [social] changes is a false one" (1966:12). This is "presence evangelism." A silent Christian presence, characterized by good works and charity, is called "evangelism." This is the basic point of disagreement.

It must be stressed that the disagreement does not arise over the need to do good works. Those who would stand firmly on the side of proclamation also affirm that good works and loving one's neighbor are essential aspects of the ministry of the church. They agree that Christian presence is necessary (1) to establish a proper identification with the people to whom the gospel is proclaimed and (2) to demonstrate the love of Christ in tangible ways which involve both material aid and social transformation. Good works authenticate the gospel. They may even produce evangelistic results as by-products when people "see your good works, and glorify your Father, who is in heaven" (Mt 5:16). But, if issues are to be kept in clear focus, doing good works should not be called evangelism. True evangelism involves as an essential (not optional) ingredient: the verbal and propositional communication of the gospel, or what we have called proclamation.

If a proper distinction is made between presence and proclamation, the first step toward a clear definition of evangelism is taken. Horner's symposium, *Protestant Crosscurrents in Mission* (1968), shows that it has been one of the crucial areas of dispute in what Horner calls the "ecumenical-conservative encounter." As Alan Tippett expresses it:

> In the final analysis, this is the one great issue at stake in all our theological and theoretical tensions with respect to the Christian mission—*what do we mean by witness?* Is it a mere Christian presence? Or is it presence which consciously strives for the conversion of men to Christ? Does witness imply a verdict? [1969:55].

PROCLAMATION VERSUS PERSUASION

In contrasting proclamation and persuasion as emphases in the definition of evangelism, we are no longer talking about differences between evangelical theology and that characteristic of much of the conciliar movement. This is simply an effort to clarify evangelical alternatives in terms of the goals they require. By sharpening these goals, we hope to clear the decks so that a meaningful foundation for missionary strategy can be laid.

Many books written on evangelism and missions assume that the reader understands proclamation to be the proper goal of evangelism. It is unquestionably the impression that a large part of the evangelical community has. Some hold this opinion without having considered the alternatives, but others hold it after having given the matter careful study.

One who has considered the options and come out on the side of proclamation evangelism is J. I. Packer of England, whose book, *Evangelism and the Sovereignty of God,* has enjoyed a wide circulation, especially among university students in Great Britain and the United States. Packer opens the dialogue by quoting the classic definition of evangelism written by the Anglican Archbishops' Committee in 1918. The archbishops' statement clearly articulates what we have chosen to call "persuasion evangelism":

> To evangelize is so to present Christ Jesus in the power of the Holy Spirit, that men shall come to put their trust in God through Him, to accept Him as their Saviour, and serve Him as their King in the fellowship of His Church [1961:37-38].

Predictably, Packer reacts to this statement by contending that it goes astray in one matter which he considers fundamental. He would prefer that the statement be more conditional, and that evangelization be defined as the presentation of Christ so that *men may come,* rather than so that *men shall come.* Packer faults the archbishops' statement by saying that "it defines evangelism in terms of an effect achieved in the lives of others; which amounts to saying that the essence of evangelizing is producing converts" (1961:40).

After rejecting persuasion evangelism as expressed by the archbishops, Packer then sets forth a clear definition of what we call proclamation evangelism as his own position:

> According to the New Testament, evangelism is just preaching the Gospel, the evangel. It is a work of communication in which Christians make themselves mouthpieces of God's message of mercy to sinners. . . . The way to tell whether in fact you are evangelizing is not to ask whether conversions are known to have resulted from your witness. It is to ask whether you are faithfully making known the gospel message [1961: 41].

With this statement Packer has touched the heart of the problem. Is evangelism merely preaching the gospel so that many hear, or does it go further and insist on bringing the hearers into a personal relationship with Christ?

We attempted to anticipate the answer to this question in Chapter 1 when we exegeted the imperatives of the Great Commission. Nowhere in the New Testament do we have a clearer command of Christ as to what He specifically considers the evangelistic task of the church to be than in the several expressions of the Great Commission. The basic imperative here is to make disciples. Going, preaching, baptizing, and teaching are all auxiliary functions, geared to making disciples. The parables describe sowing the seed only as a necessary means toward the end of harvesting the fruit. One of the dangers of defining the goal of evangelism as proclamation is that seed sowing may become an end in itself, thus blurring the vision of the fruit.

To further buttress his defense of proclamation, or seed-sowing, evangelism, J. I. Packer states that

> the question whether or not one is evangelizing cannot be settled simply by asking whether one has had conversions. . . . There have been missionaries to Moslems who laboured for a lifetime and saw no converts; must we conclude from this that they were not evangelizing? [1961:40].

Of course the answer to Packer's question all depends on your definition of evangelism. Those who hold to persuasion evangelism would say that the missionaries in question were making a noble evangelistic *effort* but nevertheless an unsuccessful one. Like some fishermen mentioned in the Bible, they were casting their nets in the water all night and had taken nothing. They may have been fishing; but unsuccessfully, since their goal was not to cast nets but to catch fish. By the same token the missionaries mentioned by Packer had not reached the goal of evangelism, that of making disciples. They had spent much time in the field, but the field they were in was not yet white unto harvest.

The dialogue continues with Packer affirming, "The results of preaching depend, not on the wishes and intentions of men, but on the will of God Almighty" (1961:41). This would be a valid argument for proclamation evangelism only if the will of God Almighty were obscure and doubtful. But God Almighty has revealed His will to us in the Great Commission—*matheteusate,* make disciples. God's will is that the lost sheep be found and brought into the fold. He desires that His banquet table be crowded, that the fishermen's nets be full. He wants seed sown not on barren ground but on fertile soil so that it will produce fruit thirty-, sixty-, and a hundredfold.

There remains little question as to the will of God Almighty. The larger question is whether God's children are willing to act on it.

Fuzziness in defining *evangelism* has a parallel, according to Ted Ward, to fuzziness in defining *communication* in general. In that field, the proclamation-persuasion dialogue sounds very much like the dialogue in the field of evangelism. Here is what Ward says:

> Carelessly used, the word *communication* refers to the process of transferring information from one point to another. The oversimplicity of this common definition conceals dozens of difficulties. Purposeful communication is more than a one-way transmission; communication is more than telling; communication is *interaction*. Purposeful communication is essentially the same process as education: the presentation of information in a carefully designed form to an appropriate audience through a useful medium in order to produce change. Notice how the definition ends: to produce change. Purposeful communication is more than *telling*; telling may or may not produce change. Until change results, we haven't gotten through—we haven't communicated (1971:90).

One could go back through this pithy paragraph, substitute *evangelism* for *communication* and come out with a most convincing case for what we have called persuasion evangelism. In other writings Ward stresses the need to be able to measure objectives in communication or education. We here stress the need to define and measure objectives in evangelism, chiefly in terms of disciples made.

Some evangelicals who generally equate evangelism with proclamation do not totally reject the persuasion emphasis. They take what may be considered an intermediate position. George Peters, for example, stresses that the aim of evangelism is definitely conversion to Christ. But he also states that when a man hears the proclamation of the gospel and takes a position *against* Christ, he is considered evangelized (1970a:20). Persuasion is called for to bring the person to a verdict, but a neutral position on results is assumed.

One of the missiologists who most clearly defends persuasion evangelism is Donald McGavran. He calls proclamation "a theology of search" and persuasion "a theology of harvest." In his defense of the theology of harvest, McGavran discusses the important point as to whether persuasion adequately respects the personality of the person persuaded. He contends that persuasion is right (1) if it is good for the persuaded and (2) if it is freely accepted. His analogy is that of a sleeping man in a burning building:

> Is it legitimate to shake him, wake him, and persuade him to leave? Certainly—even in fact if the arouser risks his own life merely for the plaudits of men or because he is paid for it. His motives have nothing to do with the legitimacy of persuasion [1970*b*:42].

A good deal of space has been given over to the proclamation-persuasion debate because it is a basic question for missionary strategy. Little of the contemporary literature on missions deals adequately with the matter. Many evangelistic programs have neglected to clarify the issue, and some of them have suffered as a result.

The apostle Paul did not shy away from persuading men as a part of his evangelistic ministry. He writes in 2 Corinthians 5:11, "Knowing, therefore, the terror of the Lord, we persuade men." He declares himself an ambassador of Christ with a forceful message: "we beg you in Christ's stead, be ye reconciled to God" (v. 20). Agrippa recognized Paul's objective when he said, "Almost thou persuadest me to be a Christian" (Ac 26:28). For Paul, proclamation was a means toward the end of persuasion.

The thought of persuasion turns some people off because they tend to confuse it with manipulation or a violation of personal rights. John White has answered this objection by carefully describing the difference between earnest persuasion and skillful manipulation:

> The manipulator is concerned with results; the persuader (assuming his attitude is truly Christian) is concerned for a person. The manipulator grows more efficient as he remains emotionally detached from his victim's personal problems; the persuader is already involved deeply. The manipulator always has an ulterior motive; the persuader need never and should

never have one. The persuader may weep as the person he talks to remains dry-eyed, whereas the manipulator is hitting pay dirt when his victim weeps while he himself remains in full control. Jesus wept over a stony-hearted Jerusalem, and Paul warned men night and day with tears [1967:13].

One of the finest recent definitions of evangelism comes from the pen of Samuel Moffett of Korea. In his carefully worded and well-balanced statement, he affirms that evangelism is preaching, it is preaching with power, and it is preaching with power for a purpose. What is this purpose?

Evangelism is the bringing of persons to Christ as Savior and Lord that they may share His eternal life. Here is the heart of the matter. There must be a personal encounter with Christ. For on this relationship to God in Christ depends the eternal destiny of man. This and this alone is the purpose of evangelism [1969:13].

EVANGELISTIC GOALS

Strategy cannot be accurately planned or effectively evaluated without measurable goals. It would be well, then, to clarify as much as possible the typical goals which emerge from each of the three definitions of evangelism: presence, proclamation, and persuasion.

Presence evangelism sets as its goal the humanization of man. Wherever people are helped to become more human, where racial barriers have been broken down, where hungry stomachs have been filled, where disease has been cured, where dehumanizing social structures have been torn down, where just social legislation has been passed, where peace has been ushered in, there evangelism has occurred. Evangelistic success is measured in terms of how many people are helped through the efforts of Christians. *Compassion* becomes the end for evangelistic work.

Proclamation evangelism measures success against the yardstick of how many people hear and understand the gospel message. This is often reported in terms of how many people are reached by attending a certain evangelistic campaign, listening to a certain radio broadcast, or reading a certain piece of evangelistic literature. *Communication* (not the kind described by Ted Ward on page 130) becomes the end for evangelistic work.

Persuasion evangelism evaluates success only in terms of how many new disciples are made, how many persons previously without Christ and without hope in this world commit their lives to Him and become members of the household of God. *Conversion* becomes the end for evangelistic work.

The best missionary strategy, in our opinion, is that which clearly articulates conversion as the evangelistic goal. This does not reject either presence or proclamation as good and necessary activities, but it does go beyond both of them in defining the ultimate purpose of evangelism. Christian presence is good; it is obedience to Christ's command to love your neighbor. But it is not evangelism in itself. Proclamation is an indispensable evangelistic tool, since faith cometh by hearing and one cannot hear without a preacher; but it is only a means, not evangelism in itself. Making disciples is the end toward which presence, proclamation, and other means should lead.

The final declaration of the World Congress on Evangelism in Berlin was careful to articulate the purpose of evangelism in its definition. It affirms that

> Evangelism is the proclamation of the Gospel of the crucified and risen Christ, the only Redeemer of men, according to the Scriptures, *with the purpose of persuading* condemned and lost sinners to put their trust in God by receiving and accepting Christ as Savior through the power of the Holy Spirit, and to serve Christ as Lord in every calling of life and in the fellowship of his church, looking toward the day of his coming in glory [Henry and Mooneyham 1967:I:6, itals. added].

THE RELATIONSHIP OF PRESENCE, PROCLAMATION AND
PERSUASION

Experience has shown that some of the people, after thinking through the options for a definition of evangelism, become overly exclusive in their position. Some get the idea that to define evangelism as persuasion implies that presence and proclamation are excluded. This is incorrect.

The properly balanced view of evangelism is what could be

called 3-*P* evangelism. The *P*s should be considered as building blocks which form a total unit of three stories. If Persuasion is the goal, it is the third story, but the third story rests on the second which is Proclamation. There is no persuasion without verbal proclamation of the gospel. But proclamation cannot be accomplished in a vacuum. The second story rests on the first, which is Presence. Presence gives relevance and credibility to proclamation. Pull out the first story of presence, and the whole structure topples down. As Paul Rees has said,

> A visible, credible Christian presence (no less than an audible Christian witness) in the factories, offices, shops, schools, villages, and farm districts will be required if masses of non-Christians are to reach a verdict for or against Jesus Christ [1971:32].

To summarize what has been said, I would like to propose a composite definition of the mission of the church as follows:

> *The mission of the church is to so incarnate itself in the world that the gospel of Christ is effectively communicated by word and deed toward the end that all men and women become faithful disciples of Christ and responsible members of His church.*

This definition is 3-*P* evangelism. It includes presence (incarnate itself), proclamation (communicate), and persuasion (become disciples). It is careful, however, not to be satisfied with only one *P* or two *P*s. The third *P*, persuasion, is always the final goal of biblical evangelism.

SATURATION EVANGELISM

Now that evangelism in general has been defined, we can move to the term *saturation evangelism,* which has been popularized by George Peters and is widely used in missionary circles. It is an umbrella term which Peters has adopted to include the many different evangelistic movements of the day which follow to one degree or another the pattern of Evangelism in Depth. No better approach to defining saturation evangelism could be found than to summarize Peters' own ideas. Although he doesn't use these exact words, he describes in order the aim, the means, the timing, and the scope of saturation evangelism.

The aim of saturation evangelism is to present the gospel in spoken and written form to every people of the land, to every stratum of society, to every home and individual, overlooking no area and no community. It comprises an in-depth evangelism program literally attempting to fulfill the command of Christ to preach the gospel to every creature (Peters 1970*a*: 39).

The means of saturation evangelism comprises an attempt to reverse the common pattern of "church centripetalism" and transform it into dynamic "evangelistic centrifugalism." The church is not to be thought of as the only place for evangelism. The time for evangelism is not only when the church holds an evangelistic campaign. Saturation evangelism seeks to mobilize and train every believer available to become an active and effective evangelizer for Christ. If the world is to be evangelized, it will have to happen outside the church buildings (1970*a*:40-41).

The timing of saturation evangelism follows a predetermined and coordinated schedule of simultaneous activities throughout all cooperating churches. This helps produce unity of spirit and depth of impact. Coordination and cooperation make the impact of saturation evangelism comparable to that of a mighty army marching through the land (1970*a*:41-42).

The scope of saturation evangelism includes as many churches, missions, and denominations as will cooperate in an evangelical and evangelistic program in order to express the unity of the body of Christ, strengthen the cause of evangelism, involve and train as many believers as make themselves available, and create the greatest possible impact upon the churches and communities (1970*a*:42).

One question frequently asked concerning saturation evangelism is whether this is something new. Strachan himself said, "Evangelism in Depth has been hailed by some as new strategy of evangelism. But in fact it involves nothing basically new" (1964:197). Whereas on one hand some critics feel that saturation evangelism is just the same old thing in larger doses, on the other hand some claim that it is a "revolution in evangelism." But whether saturation evangelism differs from the traditional variety in kind or only in degree, few question the tremendous worldwide impact that has resulted from the genius of Kenneth Strachan. Evangelism in Depth and its offspring have done more to make Christians aware of their evangelistic responsibilities than any other factor I know of in our half century.

THE PROTOTYPE: EVANGELISM IN DEPTH

It is unnecessary to describe in detail all the saturation movements now being employed throughout the world. Many excellent books are available on the subject. It will be helpful, however, to sketch briefly just what goes on throughout a saturation effort, using Evangelism in Depth as a model. My personal participation in the year-long Evangelism in Depth program in Bolivia in 1965 has enabled me to observe the operation from the inside; although I must admit that each effort, to a degree, forms patterns which are different from other similar efforts.

What now is known as the Strachan Theorem provides the theoretical basis for Evangelism in Depth. It was first articulated by Kenneth Strachan as a result of some serious research on evangelism. The conclusion that Strachan reached was stated by him as follows:

> The expansion of any movement is in direct proportion to its success in mobilizing its total membership in continuous propagation of its beliefs. This alone is the key [1968:108].

As a service organization, the Latin America Mission has made its resources available to the evangelical community in any Latin American country requesting a year-long Evangelism in Depth effort. Preliminary arrangements are made by LAM personnel with local leaders, and a national committee is organized. This committee enlists the cooperation of as many groups within the country as possible, draws up the budget, names the leaders, and sets out the schedule.

When the national movement begins, one or more LAM consultants move in for a year-long residence in the target country. Prayer cells are organized in as many homes as possible. A training program is designed to prepare every believer in his local church for personal evangelism. His teacher is usually his own pastor, who has been instructed previously by Evangelism in Depth personnel. Once the believers are trained, a month-long visitation campaign is held with the goal of visiting every house in the country. Then local evangelistic campaigns are conducted in every church, with special efforts on a larger scale for women, youth, ethnic groups, university students, and any other target population. A series of regional campaigns are held all over the country, and the climax comes with the national campaign in the capital city. After this, LAM personnel leave; and the churches move into their own follow-up programs.

Evangelism in Depth efforts held to date include Nicaragua (1960), Costa Rica (1961), Guatemala (1962), Honduras (1963-64), Venezuela (1964), Bolivia (1965), Dominican Republic (1965-66), Atlantic Coast of Nicaragua (1967), Peru (1967), Colombia (1968), Ecuador (1970), Mexico (1971), and Paraguay (1971).

OTHER RELATED MOVEMENTS

The basic concerns which brought Kenneth Strachan to the place of creating Evangelism in Depth were present also in the hearts of many other mission leaders throughout the world. Whether similar programs would have emerged if it were not for Strachan is not known. It does seem, however, that he was God's man for the moment and that the courage and insight he was able to radiate, combined with the effectiveness of the public relations network, set off a chain reaction.

One of the links in the chain was the New Life for All movement in West Africa. In the 1963 inaugural meeting of New Life for All, Gerald Swank "read excerpts from the story of Evangelism in Depth, a tremendous movement of the Spirit in Latin America with which he had come in contact while home on furlough" (Lageer 1970:11). The most complete account of this movement is found in Eileen Lageer's book, *New Life for All*. The key formula of New Life for All is:

Mobilization $\times$ Witness $=$ Evangelization.

From New Life for All emerged the Christ for All movement in the Congo. Noting such expanding interest, LAM set up an Office for Worldwide Evangelism in Depth in Miami and named such people as Willy Braun of Kinshasa and Malcolm Bradshaw of Singapore as regional representatives. LAM directors Dayton Roberts and Rubén Lores traveled around the world, sharing their experience with leaders from other countries. The Total Mobilization effort on Shikoku Island of Japan in 1969 was organized as a result. Although perhaps less traceable to Evangelism in Depth itself, the nationwide movement in Vietnam called Evangelism Deep and Wide was organized also in 1969. Philippine Christians launched the massive Christ the Only Way movement in 1971.

Many missionary programs throughout the world have included saturation evangelism in their plans for coming years. There is no doubt that the spark ignited by Kenneth Strachan in 1960 has become an influential flame of evangelism for the church at large.

8

Evangelism in Depth a Decade Later

THE END OF THE PRECEDING CHAPTER pointed out how God raised up Kenneth Strachan and how his Evangelism in Depth program has become a worldwide phenomenon. Undoubtedly, saturation evangelism, as a significant part of the strategy of missions in general, is on the rise. If this is true, it is very important for us to take a long, hard look at the Evangelism in Depth movement, now that a decade has elapsed since the first effort in Nicaragua in 1960.

Making a clinical examination of Evangelism in Depth is not a welcome task in many ways. Despite every effort to be objective and detached, any criticism of the movement is open to interpretation as an attack on personalities or as destructive of an institution. Rather than being accepted as good medicine, negative comments easily can be construed as slings and arrows. But this is far from the intention of this chapter. Evangelism in Depth has been greatly used of God in the past, and it certainly will be also in the future. But because of the vast influence it is exercising on the world of missions and evangelism in our day, it has become necessary to come to grips with it in a book on missionary strategy, dissecting it at some problem points in order to help avoid certain pitfalls in the future. If it is a fact that we all learn by experience, what have we learned from Evangelism in Depth now that we have had ten years of experience?*

*In all fairness to new leadership in the Evangelism in Depth movement, the reader should be aware that some far-reaching changes in Evangelism in Depth policy were made at a consultation held in Alajuela, Costa Rica, August, 1971. As this manuscript goes to press, however, these changes have not yet been fully publicized or implemented and tested, and therefore cannot be analyzed. In this chapter, Evangelism in Depth is discussed not as something isolated from the saturation evangelism efforts being carried on in many parts of the world but simply as the prototype. It is hoped that the changes made at Alajuela will be an improvement on the classic form of Evangelism in Depth and will blaze new trails for

THE GOALS OF EVANGELISM IN DEPTH

Those who originate and implement any movement, Evangelism in Depth included, are the only ones fully qualified to state the goals of that movement. It would be well, then, as a starting point, to search the writings of the principal leaders of Evangelism in Depth for their concept of evangelistic goals.

Throughout the writings of such men as Kenneth Strachan, Horace Fenton, Dayton Roberts, and Rubén Lores, the definition of evangelism as proclamation is fairly implicit. While Strachan, in one of the foundation articles of the movement, does not discuss the matter of goals specifically, his references to "witness," "total and complete outreach," and "every creature" point toward a proclamation emphasis. He sets forth "reaching the entire area" as a specific objective (1964:195). In his last book, Strachan recognizes that the purpose of the Christian mission is that "men be led to acknowledge Jesus Christ as Lord and Savior and thus be incorporated into the fellowship and service of his church" (1968:48-49), but he does not go on to stress the making of disciples as the specific and measurable objective of evangelism.

Horace Fenton is somewhat clearer in his proclamation evangelism emphasis. At a recent consultation in Switzerland, he said that the goal of evangelism is "the getting of the gospel to every creature. In a very real sense this has always been acknowledged as the great aim of the church" (1970:6).

With some added detail, Rubén Lores also defines evangelistic responsibility as the responsibility to proclaim.

> Evangelism is a conscientious attempt to mobilize all the Christians and their resources in a given area; to evangelize all the non-Christians of that area, reaching them as individual persons, and in all of their social structures and relationships with the whole gospel of Christ; announcing preeminently its simple *kerygma:* Christ died for our sins, was buried, and rose again; but proclaiming this message in the context of its social, ethical and ecclesiastical implications [1970:44].

effective evangelism in the coming decades. Meanwhile, any meaningful discussion of this significant movement must be based on the classic form as published and practiced from 1960-1971. As the reader will see, the principles of evangelism in the areas of theory and practice which emerge here can be studied and applied to any missionary or evangelistic strategy, old or new.

In a key book on Evangelism in Depth, Dayton Roberts expresses his concern that observers might be "looking for the wrong kind of results because they do not understand the true objectives of Evangelism in Depth" (1967:84). He does not think the movement should be evaluated solely in terms of "new members and new faces," important as these might be. Along the same line, Rubén Lores has said,

> Although the statistical results of this movement may be quite impressive, its importance is measured by other criteria which usually are not evident in a statistical analysis, and which affect the life and work of a Church for many years [1967:497].

What both Roberts and Lores are saying is that Evangelism in Depth has set both quantitative and qualitative church growth as goals. They are concerned that the quantitative, statistically-verifiable results not be considered the only basis upon which to judge the effects of the movement, but that the qualitative, more intangible results be taken into account as well.

What are these qualitative effects? According to Roberts and Lores, they include better use of mission resources in a partnership program with the national church, development of new local leaders, experience for the local church in evangelistic methods, deeper understanding for denominational leaders in their functions and planning (Lores); new zeal and boldness to speak the Word of God, change from a stagnant to a growth situation, renewed Christian stewardship, and social concern (Roberts).

When Evangelism in Depth is evaluated against such goals as these, subjective measuring devices must be used. Whether some of them have been reached or not becomes in many cases a matter of opinion. Nevertheless, the universal testimony of almost all those who have participated in an Evangelism in Depth program is that to a good degree these qualitative goals have been reached. Believers have been awakened, mobilized, and strengthened in the faith. The church has been renewed internally.

But it is another matter when we raise the question as to whether these goals, excellent as they may be, properly constitute goals of *evangelism* in the strict sense of the word. The direct aim of most of them is more to improve the quality of present believers than to make new ones. Rather than "Evangelism in Depth," might not a program with these goals more accurately be labeled "Revival in Depth"?

THE QUANTITATIVE DIMENSION OF EVANGELISM
IN DEPTH

Despite the stress placed on the qualitative church growth produced by Evangelism in Depth, quantitative factors often have been mentioned, especially in the promotional literature. There is no question that the leaders of Evangelism in Depth desire that men and women become faithful disciples of Christ. In this case (unlike the rather nebulous means available for measuring qualitative growth), quantitative or numerical growth can be measured by hard data. If we have been correct in defining the primary goal of evangelism (not revival) as making disciples in obedience to the Great Commission, it becomes appropriate for us to measure this movement against whatever data we have available.

Rubén Lores indicates that numerical growth should play a significant part in evaluating results when he affirms that through the movement a church gains new vitality "because during this year of Evangelism in Depth more conversions occur than in any other year in the entire history of Christian work in that country" (1967:497). Of course, this statement was made in 1966 before much data was available, and undoubtedly at that time the impression had been created that Evangelism in Depth had produced extraordinary numerical growth in the countries where it had operated.

More data is available now, which should be checked out and analyzed. Since this becomes a relatively objective process, we can ask ourselves the question: Has Evangelism in Depth *in fact* been instrumental in stimulating increased numerical growth in the churches which have participated?

George Peters' studies led him to state that

> from the records and statistics available there is no appreciable, immediate, and measurable acceleration in church

growth evident in most churches of Costa Rica, Guatemala, Venezuela and Bolivia in the years following the campaigns [1970a:72].

He admits that, while many of the people he interviewed spoke enthusiastically of great success, they were unable to produce the objective evidence. One mission in Honduras, for example, claimed measurable growth; but their conclusions were based on testimony and guesswork (1970:73). At the conclusion of his discussion, Peters summarizes his feelings:

> No shadow falls upon Evangelism in Depth in producing professions of faith. Our problem, however, arises when we are confronted by the baffling fact that a comparable rise in figures cannot be shown in church membership. The discovery of the fact that Evangelism in Depth seemingly does not result in substantial measurable church growth at first alarmed me; later it troubled me; and now it has grown into a deep and steady concern [1970a:74].

In my own study of the Protestant church in Bolivia, I was able to analyze the 1965 Evangelism in Depth campaign in terms of numerical church growth. The impression from personal observation during the effort itself was that the churches must have been growing tremendously. An examination of the cold facts three years later, however, showed that they hadn't (Wagner 1970:164-175). In fact the percentage of annual growth of the seven cooperating denominations for which reasonably accurate statistics were available was greater during the year just before Evangelism in Depth than it was either during the year of effort or during the two following years.

Careful projections on a logarithmic graph indicate that the total membership of the seven denominations was 27,676 in 1967. However, if the same churches had continued to grow at the rate just *previous* to Evangelism in Depth, they would have totaled about 32,000 in 1967. This does not lead to the conclusion that Evangelism in Depth necessarily *retarded* church growth in Bolivia, but it does seem to indicate that neither did it *accelerate* quantitative growth.

Malcolm Bradshaw, Director of the Office of Worldwide

Evangelism in Depth in Singapore, reviews the two studies
mentioned above in his excellent book, *Church Growth
Through Evangelism in Depth.* He concludes,

> From the point of view of church growth this is admittedly a
> perplexing picture. If one researcher's report alone came to
> the conclusion that EID in Latin America is not yet producing
> significant increase in rate of church growth we might hold
> reservations concerning the validity of his conclusions. But
> the findings of CGRILA—Church Growth Research in Latin
> America (Read, Monterroso and Johnson, 1969), Wagner
> and Peters all point in the same direction. This evidence need
> not threaten the EID movement, but rather challenge it to
> identify causes and intensify its efforts to win and incorporate
> men into congregations [1969:100-101].

Paul Enyart, in his analysis of the Friends Church in Central America finds that statistically Evangelism in Depth did
not appear to cause quantitative growth in those churches.
He says,

> It is significant to note that 1962 was the year of Evangelism
> in Depth in Guatemala. The Friends Church cooperated fully
> in this program. Reports indicate there were great blessings,
> but the number of converts reported for 1962 was less than
> the number for 1961. Furthermore, the Church showed a de-
> cline for this year which would indicate that the Evangelism
> in Depth campaign did not contribute to growth in the Friends
> Church [1970b:60].

In a later passage, Enyart affirms that the church actually
decreased by 170 members during Evangelism in Depth, and
that "the number of conversions each year following Evangelism in Depth continued to drop until 1967" (1970:137).

Edward Murphy looks into Evangelism in Depth in Colombia, using statistics gathered by the Evangelical Confederation
there. His analysis reveals that

> the cycle of increasing numerical growth that reached 14,000
> the year before (the Evangelism in Depth effort) was broken
> and dropped back to 6,000, the lowest figure since 1966. . . .
> The 1969 census thus reveals that the saturation effort has
> not yet produced an increase in numerical growth in the
> churches [1970:184].

In all fairness, it must be admitted that some churches in Latin America must be able to attribute objective, numerical growth to the Evangelism in Depth effort in their region. Victor Monterroso, in a letter to the author, confirms this with the following statement:

> We are the first ones to confess we do not have appropriate machinery for statistical measurements. The lack of such instruments does not necessarily deny numerical growth, however. Rubén Lores states that the Templo Bíblico Church in San José, Costa Rica, increased one hundred members each of the four years following E/D, and three new churches were organized during that period. What Peters refers to as "not being able to produce the objective evidence" only points out the inefficiency of the churches to keep statistics.

This has not occurred on a general scale, however, at least according to the statistics that have come to light in recent years. Murphy follows his findings with the ominous question, "Could it be true that when such a program is applied to churches that already have broken forth into good growth . . . it may smother the growth instead of pushing it up to new levels?" (1970:185).

From the point of view of mission strategy, what can we learn from the ten-year experience of Evangelism in Depth in Latin America?

THEORETICAL CONSIDERATIONS

In certain aspects, the Evangelism in Depth theory is not in harmony with the principles of missionary strategy we have been developing in this book. Without falling into an aggressive attitude and with the admission that our judgment may be erroneous at any point, it would be well to note that, in several aspects, at least a reconsideration of some of the principles might be in order.

THE DEFINITION OF GOALS

As was mentioned in the last chapter, the inexorable goal of any evangelistic program should be the making of disciples. This is the imperative of the Great Commission. Anything short of this, intentional or not, probably will show up in the results.

As Evangelism in Depth has come through to this observer, the emphasis has been laid more on the sowing of seed than on the gathering of sheaves. It has more of a proclamation than persuasion emphasis. Statistics are used frequently by Evangelism in Depth, but they stress such things as the following:

Number of prayer cells organized
Number of laymen awarded certificates of capacitation
Amount of contributions toward the budget
Number of homes visited
Number of decisions through visitation and campaigns
Attendance at campaigns
Number participating in public parades

The most meaningful statistics, those of church membership increase, rates of church growth, and increase in the number of organized churches, have not been stressed in official publications. They usually are left to those outside of Evangelism in Depth to compile and analyze.

Again, this is a matter of emphasis but a crucial point for strategy. No one involved is opposed to disciples being made, but clarity in setting this forth as the ultimate objective in evangelism is not always consistent. Dayton Roberts says, for example,

> There is no disputing the *ultimate objective* of the evangelistic task. . . . The objective, then, is to take the good news to all the world, to all nations, to all creatures, and be fairly challenged to accept the gift of new life in Christ [1967:96, itals. added].

If Roberts had substituted a phrase such as "there is no disputing the divinely-appointed means" for "ultimate objective," little fault could be found with the statement. McGavran would reply to this as follows:

> Evangelicals agree with presence and proclamation as means, but reject them as ends. . . . Let me say bluntly that mission misconceives its end when it considers either proclamation or presence its basic task [1970c:106-107].

Some men connected with Evangelism in Depth have touched on this matter, showing that they would not really disagree with what is being said here. In his 1964 Fuller Seminary lectures, Horace Fenton, for example, said, "The ultimate objective is the glory that comes to God when those whom He has loved come to know of that love when they respond to it" (1965:11). In the preface to *Latin American Church Growth*, Rubén Lores admits that one encouraging sign is the growing concern for "measuring all missionary methods by the criterion of effectiveness in adding members to the Church" (Quoted in Read, Monterroso and Johnson 1969:vii). One would hope that these viewpoints become clearly articulated, guiding principles in saturation evangclism efforts in the future.

Preliminary reports from Evangelism in Depth in Mexico indicate that quantitative church growth may become a major criterion for evaluating the effectiveness of the effort there. An official news release states,

> A report from the Rev. Rubén Ramírez president of the EID committee in Veracruz, indicates that a new congregation of 400 people and another of 800 resulted from intensive visitation carried on by members of his Bethel Church. . . . Another city in Tabasco, Emiliano Zapata, has two new congregations as a result of prayer cells [Latin America Mission, 1971].

Such reporting is a considerable improvement over counting the number of homes visited or prayer cells formed. It is goal-centered rather than activity-centered.

One of the more recent saturation evangelism movements, Evangelism Deep and Wide in Vietnam, has made quantitative growth a deliberate principle. Franklin Irwin, in a personal interview, mentioned that the Evangelism Deep and Wide leaders feel the Lord has not only told them to preach the gospel but that He expects the preaching to produce results. "Preaching the gospel to every creature was taken as a *command*," he said, "but rejected as a *goal*. The goal was souls saved, and this had to be stated in specific terms."

Addressing himself to the strategy of saturation evangelism, Edward Murphy has made the following observation, which if applied to all saturation evangelism programs, would greatly increase their effectiveness:

> Seed-sowing alone is really little more than the beginning stage in evangelism. The goal of saturation evangelism must be the multiplication of new believers and the multiplication of new churches. We must restructure our programs in the light of this goal, even if it means neglecting some other aspect of our strategy [1970:150].

THE STRACHAN THEOREM

> *The expansion of any movement is in direct proportion to its success in mobilizing its total membership in continuous propagation of its beliefs. This alone is the key.*

Through the years, the Strachan theorem itself has come in for very little discussion or reevaluation. It has been accepted as true and certainly has served well in introducing a fresh dimension, that of complete mobilization, into evangelism in many parts of the world. It may be time now, however, to ask the question, Are there any flaws in the Strachan theorem? In answer to this question, at least three areas need closer examination: the total mobilization component, the resistance-receptivity axis, and the broadcast-sowing premise.

The total mobilization component. After assessing the past failures of the evangelistic programs of the church and the seemingly disproportionate success of other groups, Kenneth Strachan came to the conclusion that total mobilization was the one factor that all growing groups had in common. He considered this the key to church growth and formulated his theorem around it. Mobilization has become so central in this school of thought that present Evangelism in Depth leaders have expressed their terminological preference for "mobilization evangelism" to "saturation evangelism." Horace Fenton insists that "the worthy goal of saturation evangelism will be achieved only as a result of the total mobilization of those forces which God has already placed within His church" (1970:6).

Elizabeth Elliot's biography of Strachan reveals how he came to his conclusion:

> Ken had carefully studied the methods of three enormously successful systems—Jehovah's Witnesses, Pentecostalism, and Communism. It was in these that he found his principle of "total mobilization" which he considered revolutionary [1968: 116].

To my knowledge, the research carried out by Strachan has never been released to the academic world for critical evaluation. No empirical evidence has been published to confirm that total mobilization was either the common denominator or the key factor in the growth of these movements. The conclusion simply has been accepted.

The experience of the Communist movement in Latin America seems to indicate that total mobilization does not always lead to success but that other equally important factors come into play. On one hand, Fidel Castro totally mobilized his forces in the Sierra Maestra in Cuba and carried out a successful revolution. On the other hand, Ché Guevara totally mobilized his forces in the Bolivian hills but was unsuccessful in bringing off a similar revolution. What were the factors that transcended total mobilization? In Cuba, President Baptista maintained an oppressive government, not providing social justice for the dispossessed; and he was disliked bitterly by the common people. In Bolivia, the social revolution already had occurred in 1952, President Barrientos was the most popular leader the country had enjoyed in decades, and the peasants Guevara attempted to reach spoke a foreign language, Quechua. Total mobilization was not much of a help to Ché under those circumstances. In Cuba it was helpful, but it is doubtful that it was the key to the growth of the movement.

Some writers have suggested that other components of evangelistic strategy might be equally as important, or more important, than total mobilization. George Peters feels that, if the dynamic concepts of "relevance of message" and "cultural adaptation" could be applied with equal enthusiasm as complements of total mobilization, it would bring Evangelism in Depth more into line with the New Testament (1970*a*:83-84). Argentina's Juan Carlos Ortíz discusses total mobilization in a recent book but concludes that, even if a church is mobilized, if the same church has not been caught on fire by the Holy

Spirit and made a place where the new converts feel wanted and at home, the church will not grow (1969:13,20).

Recent research on Latin American Pentecostalism by Emilio Willems (1967) and Christian Lalive (1969) shows that certain cultural and sociological factors have played perhaps a more important part in the growth of the Pentecostal churches than mobilization. This is not to suggest that mobilization is unimportant as a growth component, but evidently it is not the *only* one.

In order to substantiate the hypothesis that total mobilization was the key factor in the expansion of any movement, as the Strachan theorem affirms, the accurate researcher would have to produce convincing evidence not only that in successfully growing movements total mobilization was *present* but also that in nongrowing movements total mobilization was *absent*. We have no evidence that Strachan conducted his research in this manner; and if he did, it is doubtful whether the facts would have upheld the hypothesis. One would suspect that the reason the Communist party does not grow well in the United States, for example, is not because it lacks total mobilization. In spite of mobilization, other factors retard its growth. To make an imaginary case, a minority of Black Muslims could totally mobilize in Australia but produce little positive growth.

However, some movements have increased without attempt to mobilize their membership. In Africa many independent movements, such as that which gathered around Prophet Harris on the Ivory Coast in 1913, grew in unusual ways because of a single personality. In fact, David Barrett, in his analysis of six thousand contemporary religious movements in Africa, has developed a scale of eighteen factors which combine in one way or another to produce growth in the movements. Significantly, none of the eighteen relates to total mobilization (1968: 109). In Indonesia the recent people movements do not seem to be related directly to mobilization as much as to a combination of political changes and a special outpouring of the Holy Spirit.

The resistance-receptivity axis. Evangelism in Depth literature does not usually reflect a sensitivity to degrees of resistance and receptivity of homogeneous units. It seems rather to assume that it is equally desirable to employ resources on any given segment of the population.

Contemporary church growth research, however, has pointed up how crucial the resistance-receptivity axis is in evangelistic strategy. The results of this research were not available to Strachan back in 1959, but they become more abundant every year, and are readily available now. One wonders whether Strachan himself would not modify his theorem in the light of this further information. At least, one suspects that he would eliminate the statement, "This alone is the key."

Malcolm Bradshaw agrees that the Strachan theorem has been formulated in an overly general way. He discusses Anthony Wallace's concept of the "revitalization" of society as a prerequisite to growth in almost all religious movements. Wallace examines Buddhism, Islam, Communism, Methodism, Jehovah's Witnesses, etc., all in the light of this factor. Bradshaw concludes,

> Growth of movements comes when the sovereign God has prepared the way by making a culture ready for change. Church growth theory is saying that the Church must be ready to move in on the situation which God has prepared. The Strachan theorem does not explicitly allow for this factor [1969: 109].

The broadcast-sowing premise. One of the corollaries of the Strachan theorem, frequently cited in Evangelism in Depth literature, is "Abundant reaping requires abundant sowing."

In a very general sense, this coincides with what we called the "basic agricultural principle" in Chapter 2. You get no harvest if you plant no seed. But if this is carried to the extreme of postulating that the more you sow the more you reap, it becomes a weak premise. It is what may be called "broadcast sowing."

All farmers know that abundant sowing does not always result in abundant reaping. More important than the quantity, is *where* you sow. If you sow along the roadside or on rocky soil, you can sow as abundantly as you wish, and no harvest will come. Also more important than how much you sow is *how you do it.* Even if you choose your most fertile field, if you sow too much corn or if you scatter it rather than plant it in rows that can be cultivated, you will get a scant harvest. Seed sowing should be abundant (or optimum), but it must also be discriminatory if the maximum reaping is to occur. Otherwise, what Haggai says might come true: "Ye have sown much, and bring in little" (1:6).

One member of the Evangelism in Depth team who does reflect this sensitivity is Malcolm Bradshaw, who says, "The intentional planting of new churches in receptive units should be one of EID's first priorities." He suggest that "In lieu of door-to-door visitation among strangers, it might often be better to visit family and personal contacts" (1969:113-114). This is discriminatory, as contrasted to broadcast sowing. Broadcast sowing, unless clearly qualified, is a poor premise for evangelistic strategy.

In summary, the Strachan theorem contains much helpful truth. But, in the light of current missiological studies, the time might be ripe to restudy and perhaps rephrase it.

MATCHING RESOURCES AGAINST NEEDS

In Chapter 1 we discussed at some length the fallacy of basing missionary strategy on the need of a given people. An example of this is found in the promotional booklet, *New Dimension in Evangelism:*

> If evangelism is carried out haphazardly, some sections of a given city may be visited by several churches and other sections totally neglected. This has been one of the curses of our missionary activity in many areas—the lack of planning and coordination. Put very simply, the needs must be studied, the resources analyzed, and a plan developed to match the resources against the needs in a systematic way [Latin America Mission, n.d.:8].

On the surface, this sounds like reasonable strategy planning. Notice, however, the assumption that because everyone in a given city *needs* Christ (with which we agree, of course), it follows that resources should be extended equally over the city. Concentration on certain sections seems to be a "curse."

Since every man without Christ does need Him, this makes "need" a universal quality, and thereby an overly generalized criterion for strategy planning. Some more helpful and specific criterion should be elaborated. Because of the fact that resources are always limited, they should be matched to receptive units with a given geographical area, which may necessarily imply that other more resistant units receive less than an equal share. There is no more merit in "reaching" people for the sake of saying they have been reached or for "discharging one's responsibility" than there is in sowing seed where it will not grow just for the sake of sowing.

Much harvest is lost when resources are dissipated indiscriminately over unresponsive segments of the population. Such strategy could in time nullify the good effects of successful mobilization. It could cause depth evangelism to become surface evangelism. As Bradshaw affirms:

> EID, in trying to cover the whole geographical area of a country, or in seeking to "match all resources with *all* the needs and opportunities," might easily spread its effort too thin and expend equal labor upon the receptive and unreceptive alike [1969:113].

THE DISPROPORTIONATE STRESS ON UNITY

A certain degree of unity is a prerequisite for conducting an Evangelism in Depth program. While the organization does not require that every single Protestant group promise participation, certain pressures have been brought to bear so that this objective is approached as closely as possible. In a list of the basic presuppositions of Evangelism in Depth, Lores states, "Christians can and must work together in evangelism," and he goes on to cite John 17:21 as his ground: "That they may all be one . . . that the world might believe" (1970:45).

The emphasis that this gives to the spiritual unity of all members of the Body of Christ under the Head is good, and evangelicals in general need more of it. But is it not stretching the interpretation of the text somewhat to insist that for effective evangelistic strategy, a cooperative effort is needed, especially one as structured as the Evangelism in Depth program? Some of the most effective evangelistic efforts in Latin

America curiously show not only a lack of cooperation, but seem to thrive on church splits. After studying the phenomenon of "growth by splits" in Chile, Read, Monterroso and Johnson say,

> The influence of strong personalities vying for leadership has produced a proliferation of Pentecostal groups and denominations. The dynamic forces behind a newborn church create a certain spiritual momentum that results in growth [1969: 104].

One mission executive has expressed his concern over what he calls Evangelism in Depth's "triumphalism." Participants have a tendency almost to scorn the groups which, for one reason or another, choose not to participate in the nationwide effort. In Colombia, for example, the Assemblies of God decided not to participate (although they have participated in other countries). This might have been considered by some as the outcome of a narrow denominational spirit. But that was not the reason at all. In 1968 the Assemblies of God were experiencing a dramatic growth in their membership. They had developed an evangelistic strategy which was bringing in large numbers of disciples. Evangelism in Depth seemed to them to be geared more to static churches, not to growing churches such as theirs. They feared that participation in the program might well have caused them to lose their evangelistic momentum and perhaps suffer a setback. This was the true reason for nonparticipation, and a commendable one (Murphy 1970:185-186).

Some ecclesiastical tensions, deeply rooted in history, are not capable of being resolved over night. In some cases when groups that are antagonistic for one reason or another make superficial decisions to bury the hatchet for a year while the Evangelism in Depth campaign is on, they find themselves in unnatural associations which can increase tensions rather than reduce them. In one country, for example, the head of the Evangelism in Depth children's effort refused to allow the use of of the wordless book because she was not convinced that the blood of Christ should be presented so clearly to young minds. The representative of Child Evangelism Fellowship refused to obey her and used the wordless book anyway. In this case severe tensions built up because deep-seated theological differences were not erased simply by joint participation in a campaign. In another country, one denomination had to be expelled in midcampaign because one of its members, a regional coordinator, insisted on using Evangelism in Depth as an instrument to promote his own efforts for Catholic-Protestant ecumenism. Incidents such as these at least raise the question as to whether the price for outward unity might not at times be too high.

SPIRITUAL GIFTS

In Chapter 4 we stressed the matter of spiritual gifts, and the need for every member of the body of Christ to exercise his particular function. Church mobilization should gear itself to the stimulation of every member of the body to discover, develop, and actively employ the gift or gifts he has.

The Evangelism in Depth training manual does not develop this concept. It rather urges every believer to be an evangelist. Fenton remarks that, "Evangelism is the task of the whole church and not merely of a professional elite class in it" (1970: 5). This is a proper emphasis if interpreted in the right way. It is a reaction against the unhealthy professionalism that has developed in many churches, a professionalism which says that the clergy should do the work of the church, and that the laymen should be passive recipients.

The other extreme should be avoided as well, however. It is a biblical truth that God has called certain members of the body of Christ to be evangelists, if not in a professional, at least in a charismatic, sense.

It is well to keep in mind that while all Christians are expected to be witnesses, not all are evangelists. Could not Evangelism in Depth develop a clearer theology of spiritual gifts, and include this in the lay training program? As hundreds of laymen are made aware that they have spiritual gifts and begin to use them as a team, the entire body of Christ will be more active and effective in witness, and consequently more successful in evangelism.

PRACTICAL CONSIDERATIONS

Thus far, we have dealt with some theoretical aspects of Evangelism in Depth. The past decade has also taught observers many practical lessons. In concluding this chapter, we will mention five practical areas with suggestions as to how they might improve the operation of saturation evangelism movements.

RESEARCH

Bradshaw has pointed up the need for building research into the program of Evangelism in Depth. He feels that the fact that research has not yet become a significant part of the campaign preparation is a weakness of the movement. "It is doubtful whether uninformed activism will produce much growth," Bradshaw says (1969:114). He suggests thorough precampaign, midcampaign, and postcampaign research. Before the campaign, careful attention should be given to locating the different homogeneous units in a given geographical area, testing them whenever possible to discover their degree of resistance or receptivity, and directing major resources toward the most winnable people. During the campaign itself, a constant check of results against expectations and goals will provide a basis for changing the course of the campaign if necessary. After the campaign, carefully researched hindsight will evaluate returns on the investment made and suggest possible modifications for future efforts.

At the present time, the Institute of Church Growth at Fuller Seminary is one evangelical institution which has specialized in training for this type of research. Other schools will undoubtedly establish similar programs. Bradshaw suggests that Evangelism in Depth leaders should be trained at such institutions and that one or two influential missionaries and church leaders from countries preparing for future Evangelism in Depth efforts should also be encouraged to train there.

STEREOTYPING

The danger that some of the vitality of a dynamic program will be sapped away by becoming too stereotyped is widely recognized. This should be avoided in any saturation evangelism program, since this type of activity (particularly when it has been successful in one place) runs a special risk of becoming institutionalized.

During the pastors' retreat initiating the first effort in Nicaragua, the Holy Spirit reportedly fell in an unusual way, and a spontaneous all-night prayer meeting occurred to the great blessing of all concerned. In subsequent efforts, this event became programmed, and all-night prayer meetings became a part of the prescribed order. This is not to knock planned all-night prayer meetings but just to give an illustration of how easily spiritual movements can be stereotyped.

Flexibility should be allowed to a higher degree than it has so far. In some of the more recent efforts, the timing of the national campaign has been changed so that rather than making it the grand climax, it comes much earlier, and subsequent activities work back to the local churches where the follow-up work must take place. This is a commendable sign of flexibility which should characterize all saturation evangelism movements.

CHURCH PLANTING

Evangelism in Depth does not adequately stress the need to plant new churches as a specific goal. As in the case with most mass evangelism movements, it is geared basically toward making the already existing churches grow bigger. In this sense, even with all the emphasis on the churches becoming centrifugal, in the final analysis if establishing new churches is not articulated as a measurable goal, the movement will tend once again to become centripetal.

One of the most important correctives in the Evangelism Deep and Wide program in Vietnam is precisely in this area. The last page in the instruction manual shows, as a final goal, two churches in place of one, both then recycling into the continuing evangelistic program. Other saturation movements would do well to imitate this emphasis, and burn into the hearts of those who are mobilized for evangelism the need for planting new churches, and the techniques for doing it. The prayer cells could be a logical starting point for church multiplication.

An encouraging new development in Evangelism in Depth

just recently has surfaced in Paraguay, where Alberto Barrientos is overseeing the program. The instruction manual, written by Barrientos, includes an entire lesson on planting new churches. It furthermore stresses reaping rather than sowing as the evangelistic goal, deals with resistance and receptivity in a realistic way, and develops the concept of homogeneous units (Barrientos 1971:35-49). Hopefully, the critical observations relating to Evangelism in Depth in this chapter will soon be obsolete, and these principles will be incorporated in saturation evangelism programs worldwide.

The very minimum goal that should be set is for each participating church to plant one daughter church during or within a year after the Evangelism in Depth effort. This is not impossible if proper orientation and aid are given to the existing churches. According to Ebbie Smith, this is what was done in the Baptist churches in his area of Indonesia in 1967-69. Instead of Evangelism in Depth, they ran a "one plus one equals eighty" campaign. Each of the 40 existing churches was expected to plant a new one, and in the process each believer was to be duplicated. As a result their 40 churches grew to 149 and their 4,000 membership grew to 9,700 in just two years.

FOLLOW-UP

The thorny problem of how to get those who make decisions to become faithful members of the churches has not yet been solved either by Evangelism in Depth or by any of the large evangelistic movements of the day, with the possible exception of some efforts in Africa. This is still a major problem for Billy Graham, Campus Crusade, and almost anyone who has been active in evangelism. I believe that one of the greatest challenges to creative thinking and action in the church in the 1970s will be to discover the breakthrough on this problem.

Perhaps Edward Murphy of Overseas Crusades is on the right track with his outstanding essay, "Follow Through Evangelism in Latin America" (1970). For Murphy there is no evangelism that is properly planned unless follow-up is built right into the program. This is a reflection of proper goal-setting as well. If proclamation is the goal, follow-up does not have to be built in. But if making disciples is the goal, any effort is incomplete if effective follow-up is not an integral part of the program.

Evangelism in Depth leaves follow-up to the local churches. The reason for this is that since Evangelism in Depth represents no single church or denomination, it cannot actively participate in the conservation phase. An attempt is made throughout the year to prepare the churches psychologically for their follow-up responsibility, but the outcome has been no success story. The fact of the matter is that neither the Evangelism in Depth advisors nor the church leaders themselves have come up with workable ideas as to how to conserve the results.

If some group could assign top personnel to the task of finding practical ways to solve the follow-up problem, they could make a contribution to world missions equal to that made by the Latin America Mission in introducing saturation evangelism. Some kind of "Follow-up in Depth" is now needed. Perhaps a team of follow-up experts could spend year No. 2 in a given country after the team of evangelism experts finishes year No. 1. Just leaving the country altogether, and expecting the churches effectively to follow-up on their own has not borne the desired fruit.

PERENNIALISM

Unfortunately, Evangelism in Depth has not become really perennial in any of the countries I know about. This must be disappointing to Kenneth Strachan, who once wrote:

> In the final analysis, the success of the entire movement would have to be measured, not by attendance at the crusades or the number of decisions, but by the continued dynamic witness of Christians and churches [1964:197].

Part of the Strachan theorem specifically mentions the "continuous propagation of its beliefs."

In country after country, mobilization has successfully occurred during the Evangelism in Depth year, but at the end of the effort it has fallen off. Why is this?

For one thing, the majority of people who participate suffer from sheer exhaustion. The pressure of the program saps the energy from all involved. Some discontinue their regular activities to get into the Evangelism in Depth program, and afterwards they find themselves with a huge backlog of work. Some postpone their vacations and then feel that they deserve a double one. In Bolivia some leaders came out with a bad case of what might be called "evangelistic indigestion," from which it took them a full year to recover.

Holding the national campaign at the end of the year-long effort used to be a negative psychological factor. (This has now been changed.) The whole year built up to it, and it became the climax. When the national campaign was over, Evangelism in Depth was over, psychologically speaking. The program was finished. The Latin America Mission personnel sold their cars, packed their bags, and vacated their homes. The national office closed its doors. Formerly active telephone numbers produced a recorded message, "I'm sorry, this line has been disconnected." There was a general feeling that Evangelism in Depth was also disconnected, and it was time to move on to something new.

Precisely at this point, the Evangelism Deep and Wide program in Vietnam is strong. Recycling is built in from the beginning as part of the program. When the first cycle nears completion, the progress is reviewed; results are measured against goals. New short-range goals are set, and the new cycle begins as the old one ends. Since local people themselves are the leaders, no one leaves. And finally, as the last step, a new church is established which will in turn enter into its first cycle of outreach (Irwin, n.d.:11-12).

In conclusion, Evangelism in Depth and other forms of saturation evangelism are one of God's gifts to our times. They have brought cheer and strength to the churches in many lands. With these further insights now available, and the constructive suggestions of such leaders as Malcolm Bradshaw and Alberto Barrientos, a good program can be made still better for the glory of God and the advancement of His kingdom.

9

The Emerging Church in Mission Strategy

THE QUESTION is often being raised as to whether the day of the northern (he used to be called the western) missionary might be over. Now that churches have become to one degree or another indigenous to the countries which originally were "mission fields," might the whole concept of foreign missions be obsolete? Some contend that the churches in the Third World are capable themselves of doing whatever needs to be done there. If this is true, it means that there is little value in attempting to develop a missionary strategy at all. If it is not true, however, missionary strategy must be crystal clear as to what the best relationship between mission and church might be in a given situation.

A LOOK AT THE TERMINOLOGY

Most of us have come some distance from the term *native church*, but there still is a question as to whether the common terminology for the churches which have been planted on the mission fields of the world is adequate. Whereas we recognize that suggesting changes in the use of words is often a futile exercise, at least we can make an attempt to reexamine some of the current terms.

Indigenous churches is somewhat of an improvement on *native churches*, but it too is becoming worn out. In some cases it has become merely a shibboleth, meaning whatever it is that missionaries are vaguely supposed to be working towards. At times it is clumsy to translate, since in Spanish (and other Romance Languages) the literal rendering comes out as "native" or "Indian." Those who attempt to live by the precise definition usually mean a church or denomination which is owned and operated by nationals as contrasted to a missionary-dominated church. But even in this sense it can be rather ambiguous, since it would be possible for a church to be completely free of foreign ties, and yet remain as an exotic enclave with little relevance to the wider cultural context.

Younger churches as a possible description raises the question: younger than what? The Methodist Pentecostal Church in Chile is older than the Assemblies of God in the U.S.A., but even so the former is referred to as a "younger church." Even included among the "younger churches" at times is the Mar Thoma Church of India, first planted by the Apostle Thomas! Furthermore, even these "younger churches" are often busy planting new churches, whereby they themselves become "older churches." J. H. Bavinck says, "The New Testament concept of the church does not permit any profound distinction between old and young churches" (1964:194).

National churches is perhaps the most commonly used term, and it will be with us for some time to come. If taken too literally, it could sound like a synonym for *state churches*, and this must be avoided. James Scherer is correct when he says:

> The positive yet critical attitude toward national cultures cannot lead to a "national church," if by this is meant a church that is finally subservient to national interests. There can be a church *for* a nation and a church *in* a nation, but not a national church [1964:138].

The churches for which we are developing a terminology are most often gathered churches, not state churches. They are voluntary associations, separate in all ways from the state. Even when *national church* is not intended to mean state church, however, it can still have several varying connotations, such as:

It can mean a church which exists in only one nation. The *Iglesia Evangélica Peruana*, for example, considers itself a "national church" in this sense, since it is not *inter*national— it exists only in Peru.

It can mean, especially in promotional literature, a church planted by a foreign mission, and even one functionally (although perhaps not formally) under the control of the missionaries. In some situations where arrogant paternalism still reigns, reference is nevertheless made by the missionaries to their "national church."

It can mean, conversely, a church which has *not* been planted by a foreign mission, such as the Little Flock movement in Taiwan. In this case the church might consider itself "national" as contrasted to "mission related."

"The three selfs"—self-supporting, self-governing, and self-propagating—were very useful terms when mission societies were emerging from a colonial, mission-dominated relationship with the new churches. They together depicted what came to be known as the "indigenous church." But today they are rather senile terms, although the ideas behind them are still good. They might better be replaced by something more contemporary. Henry Lefever cautions against the use of these terms, since "the New Testament speaks of 'self' only as something to be denied, or at least something to be discovered only through being set aside and forgotten" (1964:16). If the three selfs are but steps toward the ultimate goal of becoming a church for others, they are helpful; but they should not be taken as goals in themselves.

With all the vagueness of terminology that plagues our attempts to describe what we are aiming toward in missions, it is unfortunate that something better cannot be done. Must we simply resign ourselves to the fact that words will continue to be used much as they are now? Perhaps we could steer toward the wider use of geographical or ethnic adjectives, such as "Japanese church," "Auca church," or "Nigerian church." As a generic term, perhaps "emerging church" or "Third World church" could parallel current secular usages of "developing nations" or the "Third World."

THREE SIGNS OF A MATURE CHURCH

All missionaries agree that one of their objectives is full maturity in the churches they plant. Just what constitutes a "mature" church?" The description we will attempt goes beyond the self-supporting, self-governing, and self-propagating categories, without denying the validity of any of them. It furthermore is not intended to be limited to the Third World, since the same signs could profitably be applied to churches in the sending countries. Mature churches can take care of themselves, they are churches for others, and they are relevant to their cultural situation.

A CHURCH THAT CAN TAKE CARE OF ITSELF

A mature church is capable of solving its own problems, and developing its own characteristic life style. It can care for itself psychologically, liturgically, spiritually, administratively, and financially. Each one of these areas bears further examination:

It can take care of itself *psychologically*. A mature church is a well-adjusted church. It is conscious of its own identity, while not being self-conscious about it. Alan Tippett calls this the church's "self image" (1969:133), and Beyerhaus and Lefever call it "responsible selfhood" (1964:64). It harbors no inferiority complex which makes it suspect that it might be a tool of foreign influences. It is neither a dependent child nor a rebellious adolescent, having left such stages of development behind. It has developed a comfortable feeling of belonging within its cultural ecology, even when still a small minority. It does not feel it has to apologize to anyone for its existence.

It can take care of itself *liturgically*. The liturgy of a mature church is not a carbon copy of that of the mother church. It has intelligently examined all things and retained the good. Few liturgical elements can be transferred cross-culturally, and still retain their deeper meanings. New liturgy must emerge from the grass-roots, since it is intrinsically culture-bound. The hymnology of the mature church reflects the national or ethnic musical idiom in a recognizable way. It combines good taste with authentic music and is able to strike the balance between reverence and indulgence. Chandu Ray suggests that

> When missionaries from western countries came to Southeast Asia, they translated the hymns from the German and English languages and paid scant attention to the power of indigenous music, which went with the dance and drama of existing cultures [1971c:1].

The homiletical style has also been freely adapted to cultural patterns in the mature church. If preaching communicates the truths of the Word of God, there is no "right" style. Only if it does not communicate is it wrong, regardless of the style.

It can take care of itself *spiritually*. The mature church, as the body of Christ, recognizes and makes use of the spiritual gifts that God has provided. It does not quench the Spirit by restricting the use of gifts, or by failing to encourage every member to be using his gift. It has the gifted men necessary to provide its own ministry for public preaching and private pastoral care. The ministry is dynamically functioning to edify Christians, providing them the spiritual food necessary for their own qualitative growth or perfection. It provides adequate biblical and theological training for its ministers. Although this often comes much later, a mature church has developed its own distinctive articulation of theology and ethics.

It can take care of itself *administratively*. The particular form of church government adopted is congruent with the culture of its members. In order for this to happen, the church must be made to recognize that the New Testament allows wide variations in church government, and does not necessarily prescribe any one structure. Others have called such administrative development "organic growth." This includes both the hierarchical structure and the method of selecting the members of the hierarchy. It does not necessarily have to emerge as a congregational government or a democratic electoral process, although such a system is useful if it makes sense to the members. Even the traditional denominational distinctives should be flexible enough to adapt to the local situation, and not imposed by the tradition of the mother church. Since the original distinctives of the mother church were most likely themselves developed through the influence of a particular cultural setting, the same orientation should not be imposed uncritically upon the new church.

It can take care of itself *financially*. The budget of the mature church is geared to the local economy. The church should be able to afford its own expenses, or else not incur them. In this area missionary paternalism and "inter-church aid" have been particularly harmful in some cases. Too much giving can create artificial "needs," such as pastors' salaries, church buildings, Sunday school quarterlies, stained glass windows, pipe organs, and other things which the church itself could not afford without a subsidy from abroad. It can also produce the negative effect of failing to teach the national Christians to give to the Lord's work, since they really never get to feel the true financial needs of their own church. Sometimes fear on the part of missionaries that they might give the impression they were making money from the gospel has inhibited them from adequately stressing financial responsibility.

A CHURCH THAT IS A CHURCH FOR OTHERS

The mature church has become neither ingrown nor introverted. It may rightly have concern for its own needs, but this concern is not all-consuming. As in human development, the infant is not expected to let the needs of others guide his behavior, but the mature man or woman is expected to do so. In spite of Old Testament emphases on bringing offerings into the temple storehouse, the New Testament passages on giving are almost without exception concerned with giving to others. Some might interpret "the laborer is worthy of his hire" as an exception, but there are few. The great passage on giving in 2 Corinthians 8-9, as well as portions of Romans, 1 Corinthians, and Philippians, all exhort the churches to give to others outside their immediate Christian community.

Many churches in the homelands have become so introverted that the field missionaries they send out are bound to reflect this deficiency to a degree. The churches which have, through faith, been able to give fifty percent or more of their income to others seem to be the churches God is blessing, and this attitude is contagious.

Social concern is another natural result of the maturing process, whereby love for one's neighbor is worked out in a tangible way. A mature church has a program of service to the community wherever human need exists. Its social concern authenticates the gospel it announces.

A mature church is successfully discipling the non-Christians in its own community. Growth comes from conversions from the world as well as from biological and transfer growth. Not only does it grow as a congregation, but the mature church sends forth people to plant daughter churches in neighboring communities. Finally, it has developed a cross-cultural vision for planting churches in other cultures, whether near or far.

This final step is one of the most advanced signs of maturity, and not yet common enough in the Third World.

A CHURCH THAT IS RELEVANT TO THE CULTURAL SITUATION

In almost all cases, relevancy seems to be a necessary counterpart to numerical growth. When a church is growing by conversions from the world, in some valid sense it must be relevant to the people it is appealing to. Justo González, for example, says:

> Practically, the claim to relevance without growth is nonsense because it is difficult to see how a body can be relevant to its situation and still not attract others who wish to join it, or at least hear its message [1969:116].

One case in point is the remarkable situation of Chilean Pentecostalism. In spite of the fact that these churches are growing steadily, they have been accused by some observers of being socially irrelevant, a "haven of the masses." Such a conclusion undoubtedly betrays an ideological bias. To some, any group that does not participate actively in the "revolution" is considered ipso facto irrelevant. González again provides an answer to this when he says,

> It is difficult to see how a movement that is totally irrelevant to the human situation can have the surprising growth that is so characteristic of Pentecostalism [1969:119].

A sealed-off church, out of touch with those around it, lacks some very important element of maturity. Since it is God's purpose for the church to be an agent of reconciliation in the world, maturity implies dynamic fulfillment of that purpose. The message of reconciliation can only be communicated effectively if it is culturally relevant. Otherwise, it will win no one.

THE ROLE OF THE MISSION AGENCY

In many Christian circles today the role of the foreign missionary agency is being played down. It is said that no longer are northern missionaries needed since the Third World church can handle its own affairs, and that missionary activity is often considered interference. Some Third World churches have literally said, "Missionary, go home!"

Much of this attitude springs from misunderstandings of the true role of the missionary and the mission agency. In this section we will attempt to defend the point of view that the mission agency, whether western, northern or Third World, is still very much needed, and will be until Christ comes. When cross-cultural missionary work is deliberately cut back, such an action reveals a basic weakness in the church. As was previously mentioned, God does not will a postmissions age in the church. For this reason, we need to take a look at some of the erroneous thinking that may have contributed to this mentality.

THE "INDIGENOUS CHURCH" AS A GOAL

The proper goal of the Christian mission is not to establish an "indigenous church." While saying that, I am aware that many will misunderstand me; but I will attempt to explain the matter carefully. It is not meant to imply that churches must not be formed as an essential part of accomplishing the true goal of missions. They certainly must, but even planting churches is only a means toward another end. As we have repeated scores of times in this book, the true goal of missions is making disciples.

Disciples are not made in the church, as indigenous or mature as that church might be. Disciples are made among unbelievers who are not yet members of the church. If we do not keep this clearly in mind, the establishment of a church is likely to become thought of as an end in itself, and once a solid church is established and organized by disciples already made, the mission agency might begin to lose its original vision for reaching those who are not yet disciples.

The indigenous church, we repeat, is best seen, in terms of strategy, as nothing more than a recycling phase of disciple making. The function of the church involves bringing disciples together in fellowship for worship, mutual exhortation, and spiritual edification. These things are all good, and they glorify God. Disciples should spend much time worshipping God. But this worship must never be in isolation from evangelistic outreach to those without the fold who should also be worshipping God, but who will not do so until they become Christians. Worship should only be a meaningful pause in the continuous process of recycling evangelistic efforts.

The danger of losing this focus on the true goal of missions is ever present. Lefever says,

> A Church which feels that its own responsibility has been discharged when the new Church is established as a self-governing, and wholly or largely self-supporting body, has never rightly understood its missionary responsibility [1964:12].

A missionary from Cameroon once told me that a mission he knew of was so devoted to "indigenous principles" that when they heard of a new, receptive tribe which wanted to hear the gospel, the missionaries refused to go on the grounds that it was now the responsibility of the Cameroon church. The Cameroon church, however, was not prepared to undertake the task. Among other things, its members were traditional tribal enemies of the seeking group. Turning this task down seemed to be the ideal action for the mission, but many years have gone by and nothing has yet been done. This illustrates a case of carrying "indigenous principles" too far. When they interfere with completing the Great Commission, thus preventing some men and women from being reconciled to God, they should be scrapped without ceremony. Charles Kraft warns against "indigenization becoming merely a mask for irresponsibility" (1971:7). Indigenous principles, after all, are only a means, not an end in themselves.

THE SYNDROME OF CHURCH DEVELOPMENT

The "church development syndrome" is an outgrowth of the confusion of goals in missionary work. Very slowly and very subtily, some missions have been twisting priorities. Whereas they once began with a vision of discipling the nations, they now have fallen into the trap of placing exaggerated emphasis on the development of the new church. Energies formerly invested in evangelism are now diverted into well-intentioned efforts to direct the inner spiritual and organizational growth of the church. They have left off "baptizing them in the name of the Father, and of the Son, and of the Holy Spirit" and have begun to devote themselves exclusively to "teaching them to observe all things whatsover I have commanded you."

Instructing new believers is absolutely necessary, of course. The sheep need pastoral care if the wolves are not to snatch them away. But pastoral care is not intended to *replace* evangelism; it is intended to *supplement* it. The attention of some missionaries has been so drawn to the fascination of seeing the young church begin to move forward on its own that this has become their exclusive interest. It is almost like those young couples who pay an exaggerated amount of attention to their new baby, allowing their own lives to become much too intimately involved with the child. The ultimate loser is usually the overly coddled child.

This is why the biblical goal should not be blurred by previous successes. As Ralph Winter says,

> Some agencies of mission are so enthralled by the new fact of the younger church that they . . . focus nonpaternalistically and "responsively" on the one sheep that has been found rather than on the ninety-nine that are still lost [1971*b*:12].

If the missionary has set the perfecting of the emerging church as his *ultimate* goal, he may not only lose hold of his first love (that of reaching the lost), but he also runs the serious risk of *harming* the church with an overdose of paternalism. Paternalism will not bring a church to perfection.

This is not to oppose helping an emerging church in key areas such as ministerial training, theological development, literature, radio, and other fields which may represent more advanced stages of growth. It is to warn, however, against so strong an emphasis on this good and necessary missionary work that evangelism tends to take a back seat.

George Peters sees mission institutionalism as a part of the problem. He writes the following from Africa:

> Missions and churches who place evangelism first are reaping abundantly, doubling every three or four years. The tragedy of the situation is that most evangelical missions are so overloaded with institutionalism that it becomes practically impossible to free personnel for the ministry of evangelism. Of course, the argument is that the national church is to evangelize. This sounds logical and easy. However, this raises two serious questions: Are we still "missions?" Have we not ceased to be missions and become a service agency? Again,

how does this speak of our priority? . . . A wrong sense of priorities is also developing in the churches. As missions "retreat" into institutions, so the national church, consciously or unconsciously, desires to do so [1970*b*:2].

Good strategy will not neglect the development of the church, but neither will it allow missions to become so deeply enmeshed that the church itself resents the mission and says, "Missionary, go home!" When missionaries are out on the growing edge, bringing unbelievers to Christ, organizing them into congregations, and handing over the new churches to the denomination, few national leaders are going to tell *that* kind of missionary to go home. Mission agencies dedicated to fulfilling the great commission should keep their vision fixed on the 95 percent who are not yet Christians, without allowing themselves to become overly sidetracked by the 5 percent who are.

THE PERENNIAL NEED FOR THE MISSION

What has been said so far indicates that mission agencies today should not consider their task accomplished, nor should they even plan on cutting back. As long as there are two billion men and women in the world today without Christ, multitudes of whom are receptive to the gospel, we need more, not fewer, missions and missionaries. Peter Beyerhaus says,

> As to the extent to which missionaries from the older churches should serve the younger churches, the words of Matthew 9:38 are still valid: "Pray ye therefore the Lord of the harvest, that He will send forth laborers into His harvest." There cannot be any excess of missionary service if it really restricts itself to spreading the Word and "seeketh not its own" [1964: 173].

Many missionaries have casually made the statement: "Our responsibility is to work ourselves out of a job." This is valid if it refers to jobs related to internal church development. But it can be misleading if it refers to evangelistic work. It gives the idea that world missions are only temporary or stopgap, and that eventually churches may not have to send out any more missionaries. This is unbiblical and unrealistic. The need for missions (including, of course, missions from the Third World churches as well as northern missions) is perennial.

The emerging church itself needs good examples from the missionaries if it is going to develop in a healthy way. If missionaries consistently say, "We are not going to evangelize because this is the responsibility of the national church," they may contribute to a vicious cycle which could result in a Third World church with no missionary vision. If the mission leaves its first love, it can hardly expect the church it plants to do any better. Such a policy can be interpreted by nationals to mean that the mission regards soul-winning as a secondary priority. Although it may be an overstatement, an Uruguayan churchman expresses a typical Third World reaction as follows:

> We recognize the sacrificial labor which the pioneers undertook, spreading the message of the Gospel throughout those first years of American independence: the difficult sacrifice, the impassable roads they had to travel, and the hardships of all descriptions. But today the situation has changed in several aspects. As to function, the pioneers had only one objective: to win souls; and they struggled bravely toward this end in spite of the fact that they did not have the means we have now. . . . Missions today, however, are different. The majority have become nothing more than fund raising agencies, and the chief concern of the missionaries is to receive their salaries [Tahmazian 1969:3].

If we grant that this is a caricature, we should also grant the fact that much missionary work done today does appear in such a light to many national leaders. The more we fall into the "church development syndrome," the more this distorted image is likely to increase.

Some of the Third World churches are doing a magnificent job in evangelization. Many are too busy winning souls to spend much time on internal missionary-national tensions. Others, however, are static and introverted, doing very little in effective evangelism. When the latter is true, and especially when the churches tell the missionary to go home, the mission agency is face-to-face with a most difficult decision: Should it obey the church and withdraw, or should it move out to the whitened harvest fields even without the blessing of its daughter church? Perhaps the counsel of Bishop Stephen Neill is apropos:

> If an older Church seems to hear a clear call to evangelize, it may be necessary that it should go forward leaving the younger Church to follow when it is sufficiently awake itself to hear the call [1967:165].

Along the same lines, and lamenting the decision of a large mission board to withdraw missionaries from Ethiopia in order to "Ethiopianize" its program, Arthur Glasser writes,

> The Church Growth movement is deeply committed to the indigenization of the churches. But it has never endorsed the automatic reduction of western personnel for theoretical reasons, especially from a country at a time when people have never been so winnable and when doors have never been so open to their contribution [1971c:116].

MISSION-CHURCH RELATIONSHIPS

This brings us to the heart of the debate. Let us grant for the present that missions should continue to function. In a given country, then, should the mission plan to continue its independent and autonomous organizational existence parallel to the emerging church, or should it eventually be absorbed by the church, and work under the church?

The basis for decision here is really not so much a biblical and theological matter as it is pragmatic and functional. One could deduce from the spiritual unity of believers in the body of Christ that the visible unity of church and mission should reflect it. This argument, of course, would apply equally to the union of different churches within or without a given country, and indeed is a theological basis for the ecumenical movement. But many have not been impressed with this argument when balanced against other equally important biblical principles. Some feel that overstressing structural unity might inhibit obedience to the Lord's commands in other areas of activity.

In terms of missionary strategy, the central question becomes: which church-mission relationship will best enable all concerned to fulfill the Great Commission in a given situation? The answer is a complex one, and it cannot be universalized.

Denominational societies, because of their rather rigid "vertical" structures and their prescribed relationship to their new counterparts in the Third World, have generally flowed into the stream of eventual merger, bringing the mission under the full control of the national church. Such terms as "fraternal workers" reflect this posture. The interdenominational boards have not been all of one mind on this matter, but a good number of them have chosen to maintain their "horizontal" structure alongside the emerging church and not bring themselves under the newly-formed vertical structure on the field. Cooperation and partnership are usually watchwords.

At times the decision becomes uncomplicated because of national law. In Congo, for example, fusion of mission and church is required by the government. Even the Christian and Missionary Alliance, which has held a strong policy of organizational separation of the mission and the emerging church, has had to fuse in the Congo.

Some representative opinions on both sides of the church-mission debate follow:

Henry Venn of the Church Missionary Society said about one hundred years ago:

> The *euthanasia* of a mission takes place when a missionary surrounded by well-trained Native congregations under Native Pastors, is able to resign all pastoral work into their hands, and gradually relax his superintendence over the pastors themselves, till it insensibly ceases; and so the Mission passes into a settled Christian community. Then the Missionary and all Missionary agencies should be transferred to the "regions beyond" [Warren 1971:28].

Venn is known as one of Britain's principal missiologists. He was secretary of the Anglican Church Missionary Society around the middle of the last century. His view of "euthanasia" was developed as a necessary safeguard against destructive paternalism, an avant-garde piece of thinking for those days of expanding colonialism. Venn advocated the mercy killing of the mission in an evangelized area where the church had already been successfully planted, but significantly not the euthanasia of the mission society itself. In quaint terminology, he was advising the mission to keep itself out of what we have called the "syndrome of church development."

Paul Rees of World Vision International takes this point of view:

> Some form of parallelism may serve as a temporary measure but it is not the wave of the future. It is the gurgle of the past. Neither continuing parallelism nor planned withdrawal is what the Asian and African Christians want from the missionaries. They want integration, membership, the kind of mutual commitment that makes of twain one [1969:48].

Albertus Pieters wrote from Japan in 1912 as follows:

> The American churches hold their commission to evangelize Japan, not from the church they have themselves called into being, but from a much higher source. Their responsibility to perform it does not continue through and in cooperation with the church . . . but independently of it, a responsibility to God alone [Fulton 1968:67].

Louis King of the Christian and Missionary Alliance states his position in these terms:

> In the delicate and essential problem of partnership with the national church, the Society makes a distinction between the foreign mission and the church; and this distinction should not be ignored. The mission is not a church and it exercises no ecclesiastical powers. In its relation to the indigenous church, the mission is an organized body of friends who stand ready to help when needed. Beyond the ministry of the local church, the mission must continue to function in a widening outreach. The development of the church, often beginning with a relatively small body of believers in a country, should not hinder the initiative of the missionary body composed of men and women who have been called of God to preach the Gospel to every creature [n.d., n.p.].

C. Darby Fulton of the Presbyterian U.S. Church has expressed these thoughts in *Evangelical Missions Quarterly:*

> The key word is cooperation—a mutual recognition of the autonomy of each, and a resolute mind to work in harmony of purpose and program. The functions of the two bodies are different. The mission is not a church. It does not engage in ecclesiastical control. It therefore offers its services to the national church . . . by presenting itself as a task force [1968: 74].

Such a divergence of opinion (and the list could be multiplied) only points up what many missionary leaders have been saying: the matter of church-mission relationships is the principal missiological issue of the 1970s.

FROM MISSION TO CHURCH TO MISSION

No mission which maintains the vision of the lost will be content with going out of business after the new church is established. The goal goes beyond the church to those still lost, and for that reason the mission is still needed. The task should not be considered completed, then, as long as the Great Commission still needs to be obeyed.

Four major phases of the progress of missionary work can be distinguished. The purpose of this section is to stress phase 4. The first three phases are quite commonplace in missionary literature.

Phase 1. The mission goes out to a group of non-Christians to evangelize and plant churches. The gospel is preached, converts are baptized, and the church is organized. The mission controls all of the work at this stage, since there is no alternative.

Phase 2. The mission works at church development, "teaching them to observe all things whatsoever I have commanded you." This is the first stage of organic growth in which responsibilities are shared but turned over to the national church as rapidly as possible. The mission controls less but still guides the process.

Phase 3. The mission becomes a consultant. The new church is autonomous, caring for its internal matters. At this phase the mission may choose to give up its self-identity and fuse with the church, working under the church leadership. On the other hand, it may choose to work parallel to the church, maintaining autonomy and carrying on a complimentary program in agreement with the church. But withdrawal (such as Henry Venn suggests) should not be considered a proper option at this time—not until phase 4 is operating.

Phase 4. The church launches a mission. This is the real goal, but one that has been somewhat neglected. When the missionary vision reaches only as far as phase 3, it is myopic.

Not nearly enough missionary strategy has been planned in terms of phase 4. Missions have seemed to be a necessary activity of the churches in the sending countries, but for some curious reason not too necessary in the emerging churches. A Chinese Christian leader, Chua Wee Hian, has accurately discerned this problem and has spoken out concerning it. He says,

> Most of my missionary friends confess that they have never preached a single sermon on missions to the young churches. . . . The same failure is evident in the Asian theological seminaries and Bible schools. I do not know of any school that includes courses on missions in its curriculum. No wonder Asian pastors trained in their seminaries are not missionary minded [1969:11].

Chua is right, and his observation applies to Africa and Latin America in principle. Fortunately, the trend seems to be reversing, at least among the Chinese. In the Chinese Congress on Evangelism held in Taipei in 1970, the matter was thoroughly discussed, and the following resolution was taken: "A worldwide vision in evangelism is imperative to the Chinese churches. We must become *sending churches* after one hundred and sixty years of receiving."

The Christian and Missionary Alliance already has helped their churches organize an Asian Missionary Fellowship (Mangham, 1972). The newly formed China Evangelical Seminary has included in its curriculum such courses as Christian Missions, Principles and Procedures in Church Growth, Mission Across Cultures, and Case Studies in Church Growth. The Evangelical church of West Africa, with the encouragement of the Sudan Interior Mission, has launched an effective missionary program with one hundred African missionary families on the field (Hay, 1972).

Phase 4 cannot be overstressed in missionary strategy. Missions by their very nature should be experts in the organization of new missions, and should share this expertise with the emerging churches. First of all, the missionary vision needs to be communicated to them. This can only be done if the missionary society retains its own vision for the lost in word and deed, and avoids becoming too deeply involved in the "church development syndrome." New missionary societies probably would best be formed as voluntary or "horizontal" agencies within the new churches rather than operate as a part of the "vertical" ecclesiastical structure. The Church Missionary Society in the Anglican Church and the World Mission Prayer League in the Lutheran Church and the Jesuits in the Catholic Church are illustrations of how such a structure can operate. Ralph Winter now calls these horizontal structures "sodalities" and the vertical structures "modalities." He contends that the modalities need to be sprinkled with such sodalities for good church health (1971*b*). In our terminology, he is advocating phase 4 as a necessary part of missionary strategy; and he makes the further suggestion that the most viable relationship for the future may be a mission-mission relationship in addition to mission-church or church-church (Winter, 1972).

German missiologist Peter Beyerhaus also advocates a phase 4. He says,

> The ultimate aim of missions is no longer the organizational independence of the young church [phase 3]; it is rather the building up of a Church which itself has a missionary outreach [1964:167].

One of the most eloquent contemporary appeals for phase 4 has come from the pen of Peter Yuen of the Discipleship Training Center in Singapore. His words will provide an appropriate conclusion to this chapter:

> The day for the Acts of the Asians is at hand! As Western missions have been establishing the Asian Church, now the Church in Asia must become mature in Christ, determine her God-given mission, and act—this ultimately meaning the reaching out to the regions beyond, envisioning the evangelization of the world. . . .
>
> The Western mission organization's best contribution to an Asian foreign missionary movement might well be to offer its wealth of experience to enable the Asians to establish their own foreign missionary agency. An indigenous sending agency is part and parcel of an Asian missionary church [1970:7, 11].

10

Strategy for Urban Evangelism

CITIES HAVE EXISTED from the very beginning of mankind. But never before in human history have they been as important as they are today or as they will be in the future. Present rates of urbanization are swelling cities beyond all proportion. Harvey Cox says, "Future historians will record the twentieth century as that century in which the whole world became one immense city" (1966:273). Behind this rather hyperbolic, but vivid, statement lies the statistic that by the year 2000 some 60 percent of the population of the world will be urban. It is said that in India alone, the year 2000 will see twenty cities of over twenty million each!

THE STRATEGIC IMPORTANCE OF CITIES

Cities must play a major part in planning the strategy of missions, simply because this is where the people are. One of the high rise apartments in Hong Kong could house about one hundred Auca tribes in a single building! But the number of people alone does not make the cities strategic. More important, some of the most responsive segments of population are found there, and for this reason they deserve high priority for missionary resources.

This fact, if taken seriously, may cause a shift in priorities for some missions. In making their study of Brazil, Read, Monterroso and Johnson calculated that over two hundred fifty missionaries were working among the 136,000 tribespeople of the Amazon basin. This led them to make the following comment:

A comparable investment in any of the large cities of Latin America devoted to the effective communication of the gos-

179

pel could produce more church growth in six months than would result from the evangelization of every member of dozens of jungle tribes [1969:303].

While the authors would not suggest that tribespeople be neglected or that they should not hear the gospel, they would attempt to dramatize the strategic importance of the cities in our day.

Not every city is receptive. Cities themselves can be located along a receptivity-resistance axis. To take some well-known examples, Sodom would fall on the resistant pole, while Nineveh would be on the receptive. In the New Testament, Athens would be closer to the resistant pole than Antioch.

A newer city is usually more receptive than an older city. A growing city is usually more receptive than a static or declining one. A native city, strongly animistic, would be more receptive than a colonial city with vested interests in the religious status quo. A cosmopolitan city with much commerce is more often more receptive than a provincial one. Undoubtedly, future church growth research will uncover many factors which will provide us with more accurate indications as to the fertility of urban soils for the gospel.

Not only do cities differ from one another, but within themselves they are complex patchworks of many different kinds of people. Some of the patches are responsive to the gospel; some are highly resistant. In order to plan intelligent missionary strategy, the precise configuration of each city must be plotted beforehand as accurately as possible.

To divide the city into equal parts on a map and to assign one of the sections of the map to a particular church or team of workers is a relatively unproductive way of approaching urban evangelism. Geographic divisions mean little in comparison to the distinction between homogeneous groups of people.

The most meaningful way of dividing a city map for strategy is on the basis of ethnic groups including differences in color, culture, language, and religion. The sections containing the older rich and the aristocratic city fathers should be marked. The new rich and the working class areas must be distinguished. Perhaps the most important group to locate is new arrivals. A strategy map should plot the areas where immigrants are settling, distinguish national and ethnic backgrounds among them, and indicate the time of residence in the city. The person who successfully draws this kind of map of a given city has in his hand one of the most important keys to urban evangelism imaginable. This, combined with the power of the Holy Spirit working through consecrated lives, could sweep multitudes of urbanites into the Kingdom of God.

TYPES OF CITY CHURCHES

Cities which already have Christian populations contain many different kinds of churches. The division among them is usually not so much denominational as in style. Each kind of church has its own characteristics and also its own potential for future growth, or for planting new churches. At least five general types of urban churches can be described:

THE CATHEDRAL

The cathedral is the big church in the center of the city. Typically it is an older church with a membership of mature Christians. The *traditional cathedral* represents the church of the original settlers or colonists. It would be a Congregational church in Boston, a Dutch Reformed church in Djakarta, a Roman Catholic church in Paris or an Anglican church in Sydney. Sometimes it is a state church, enjoying special privileges from the government. As a general rule, the traditional cathedral church is a nominal one, concerned about maintaining social status with the general public.

Another kind of cathedral church has entered into many cities where the traditional cathedral has existed already. This *newer* cathedral is typically the headquarters of a denomination and is located in the capital city. Often it is quite different from the majority of churches in the denomintaion, such as the case of the Maranatha Church of the *Iglesia Evangélica Peruana* in Lima. The Maranatha is a respectable, well-scrubbed, middle-class church, whereas the rest of the denomination is proletarian and largely rural. One the other hand the Jotabeche Church in Santiago, Chile, which can seat 15,000, is an active, working-class church differing only in degree but not in kind from the other Methodist Pentecostal churches in Chile. In

Saigon, the Christian and Missionary Alliance International Church caters to a congregation largely English-speaking, while across town the Vietnamese Church has its large cathedral. These are all cathedral churches of one kind or another.

THE STORE FRONT CHURCH

The store front church is usually located in an area of the inner city undergoing social change. The members are largely newcomers to the area, low on the economic ladder. Commercial patterns are changing, leaving business properties plentiful and rent low, thus making them available to small church groups. Many areas of this kind enjoy a high potential for church growth.

THE OUTER-CITY OR SUBURBAN CHURCH

Members of the outer-city churches usually live in the area immediately surrounding the church, in contrast to the members of the cathedral church, who may commute long distances to the services. The radius of influence of this kind of church depends on the type of transportation available to the average member.

Some outer-city churches have low growth potential. They once were in touch with the people of their community, but the community has changed socially and perhaps ethnically, while the church membership has stayed the same as before. The church has become sealed-off from the community and has little prospect of anything but decline. The children of members marry and move out of the community, reducing the possibility of even biological growth.

Other outer-city churches have high growth potential. Their members identify socially, economically, and ethnically with those of the community. This is often the case in ethnically homogeneous neighborhoods such as some of the African cities are developing. Certain districts have become virtual tribal enclaves, a potential problem for political leaders, but a good situation for wise church planting.

THE HOUSE CHURCH

Some have discovered that a specially constructed building

is not necessary in order to have a church. One of the larger houses belonging to a hospitable Christian family can become a church itself. In cities like Lima where it doesn't rain, or during certain times of the year in other cities, the yard or patio can be used effectively. Often the house church will continue to function until the church membership and consequently the economic possibilities of the congregation rise to the point where they can afford a lot and a church building. Until then, house churches should be considered as legitimate churches, if they have the required membership.

In a penetrating essay, Alberto Barrientos of Evangelism in Depth calls into question the necessity of any building at all. He warns that the very act of investing money in a church building may retard healthy church growth. He is rightly disturbed that instead of obeying the Lord's command to go, many churches remain comfortably seated and say, impersonally, "Come to our building." He reminds his readers of the New Testament references to house churches and then says, "Doctrinally and historically, buildings called temples are neither characteristic of New Testament Christianity, nor are they a vital factor in Christian development" (1970:6).

THE ETHNIC CHURCH

The ethnic church is one which serves the immigrants from another culture. Usually the language is that of the settlers, and little effort is made to disciple those outside the immigrant community. In areas of rapid acculturation, such as the Europeans in the United States, these churches usually begin to decline in the second generation and come to a crisis situation in the third. They will not grow for long. Where acculturation is slower, such as among Spanish-Americans in the southwestern United States, the churches have a high growth potential, especially if kept relevant to their own subculture.

MASS EVANGELISM AS URBAN STRATEGY

Undoubtedly the most commonly accepted strategy for evangelizing urban populations has been the citywide, mass evangelistic campaign. This term usually implies an effort to secure the cooperation of the maximum number of churches (either interdenominational or intradenominational), hiring an outside evangelist to do the preaching, training laymen as counselors, organizing a united choir, printing and distributing propaganda, visiting door-to-door, renting a neutral hall or stadium, holding meetings every night for a week or two, and conducting a follow-up program.

Some mass evangelistic campaigns have been successful, some not so successful. In terms of mission strategy, it would be well to analyze this particular evangelistic method.

The timing of a mass evangelistic crusade is one of the crucial inputs. When properly timed, this approach has resulted in church growth. Mass evangelism is an invasion tactic; but as any military officer knows, invasion tactics are appropriate only under certain conditions.

The Tommy Hicks campaigns in Buenos Aires in 1954 were an example of a well-timed and successful use of mass evangelism. This was the turning point in church growth not only for the Assemblies of God, but also for other denominations. In fact they "broke the back of the rigid Argentine resistance to the Evangelical witness" (Read, Monterroso and Johnson 1969:381). The campaign was not premeditated in this case; it emerged from a direct call of God to Tommy Hicks in Spokane, Washington. Buenos Aires was a ripe field at that moment, and God sent forth His harvester. The religious atmosphere was still pre-Vatican II, so invasion tactics were called for. Perón was in power, and the country was passing through a period of national optimism. Enns (1971) discusses many other aspects of the Tommy Hicks campaign.

Almost twenty years later, the pattern of church growth in Buenos Aires has become quite different. It is doubtful whether Tommy Hicks, with the same sort of crusade, would enjoy equal success. The pastor of one of Buenos Aires' largest and fastest-growing churches, Juan Carlos Ortíz, would not favor mass evangelism over other methods that he is using successfully. Probably in Buenos Aires invasion tactics are no longer called for, but in scores of other cities they might well be.

Some have suggested recently that longer campaigns have more permanent effects than shorter ones. The successful Foursquare Gospel Crusade in Guayaquil, Ecuador, in 1962 lasted six weeks. Many converts had received some large portions of the milk of the Word before it was over, and 1,500 candidates were ready for baptism at the conclusion (Weld 1968:62-63).

The Guayaquil campaign had more than timing going for it. Observers say that the divine healing aspect was important, too. This is a suspicious quality to many of the more traditional churches, but as Read, Monterroso and Johnson say, "Non-Pentecostals will have to decide whether to unite with Pentecostals in city wide healing meetings, which will doubtless continue to draw large crowds" (1969:381). More openness on this matter of healing might be helpful to many of us.

An inherent, but little-recognized, danger in city wide campaigns is that they become compulsive. Participating churches can come to feel that they must have a city wide campaign once a year, or they are not properly evangelizing. The problem is obvious. If, say, April becomes the month for evangelism, the churches can fall into the trap of saying during the other eleven months, "We are free to do other things now; we've finished our evangelism for this year."

A compulsive yearly campaign also can be poor stewardship. If it is a regular fixture on the church calendar, it is easy to forget to measure results against investment. The excitement and whirl of the activities associated with the campaign are often considered enough return on the investment, without an objective evaluation as to the permanent effect of the campaign on the churches. Activity becomes an end in itself. Socially it is a success since believers from different churches have the opportunity for fellowship in work and worship, but the question as to the "fruit which remains" often is not even raised, at least in a very loud voice.

Where should these crusades be held? Holding them in a neutral place often turns out to be a negative influence for follow-up. Most people who have been involved in this type of evangelism agree that the follow-up is the most difficult aspect of the entire effort. People who do make decisions for Christ do not always associate their action with the need of joining a church because no church is in sight at the time. When decisions are made in the church itself, or when the convert is taken to church shortly after his decision, follow-up is more successful.

Building in the goal of multiplying new congregations and churches has been another neglected aspect of planning for mass evangelistic campaigns. Although it will later be mentioned in more detail, those who are planning strategy for city wide campaigns would do well to think not only in terms of more members for the existing churches but to give equal emphasis to the deliberate planting of new churches.

Much more research needs to be done on the effects of city wide campaigns on urban evangelism. Studies now available give us only a collection of hints as to how this method might be better adapted to our cities for the goal of making disciples.

Problems of the Inner-City Cathedral

The cathedral type of church is a special problem to many Christian workers. It exists and cannot be ignored, so it must be dealt with. Unfortunately, when it is a nominal sort of church, static and evangelistically inert, it can become a drag on the whole denomination. Since it is the prestige church, its example is frequently imitated by others, and it cannot afford to set a bad example. What can be done to revitalize it?

Several characteristics of the downtown cathedral need to be understood. For one thing, there is little feeling of neighborhood solidarity among members. Fellowship stops after the ritual handshaking at the church door. The members leave for their homes in different parts of the city. Week-night services are usually poorly attended. The pastors find it difficult to visit church members regularly, and mutual visitation among members is not common either.

Because they are not under much community pressure to do so, members can attend church or not; and often their absences are not even observed. Anonymity helps create nominality. The members typically have little interest in the activities of other churches in the denomination, to say nothing of churches of other denominations.

The cathedral church is often an ethnic hodge-podge. It is a cross section of the ethnic composition of the city. This is advantageous in one way, since it demonstrates to the world the unity of different people in Christ. But new converts often get turned off by feeling they have to make an unnatural attempt to mix socially with people they have not yet learned to love. They either fall away or find a church home more congruent with their social attitudes. This is why much of the growth of a typical inner-city cathedral is by transfer rather than by conversions from the world.

The pulpit ministry of a downtown cathedral is perhaps more crucial than in other kinds of churches. Since urban people are more anonymous than their country cousins, they have more freedom to pick and choose the church they will attend; and they even feel some reluctance to involve themselves too deeply with any one church. Often their decision as to where to attend will depend on what they receive from the pulpit.

How can a cathedral church grow? This is a key question for urban missionary strategy. Efforts have been made to answer it through the years both in theory and in practice. Some inner-city churches are growing, but they seem to be the exception. Four possible approaches have and can be taken toward stimulating growth of cathedral churches.

1. *Multiplying invitations.* Some churches have operated on the principle that the way to make their churches grow is to invite more people. The pastor habitually admonishes his people, "Bring your friends and relatives to Sunday School. How many will bring someone else next week?" But while inviting people to come into a cathedral church may produce good attendance for an occasional special event, it rarely will bring appreciable results in terms of disciples made. Such invitations to an outer-city church, on the other hand, might bring good results.

2. *Multiplying activities.* The admonition to become "centrifugal" has induced some churches to begin to move out in increased evangelistic activity. This in itself is good, but it often becomes just another round of increasing invitations. Some hold open-air meetings, but they build in no direct tie with the church. At the end of the meeting the listeners are given a piece of literature and invited to come to church. Visitation programs and census-taking bring church members in contact with unbelievers, and some hear the gospel and accept

Christ. But again, a major purpose of the visitation is to invite people to come to church. Evangelistic campaigns, tracts,
literature, radio, and many other good, evangelistically oriented activities reach people; but many of them unfortunately
end up simply in more invitations to come to church. Churches
that multiply evangelistic activities run the risk of thinking of
themselves as evangelistic churches, whether or not people are
actually coming into the kingdom of God.

3. *Multiplying members.* Even when the evangelistic outreach of a church is successful in making disciples, a certain
danger is involved in expecting the cathedral church itself to
grow fantastically. There is a fallacy here. Somewhere, most
ordinary urban churches have an optimum point at which new
members start to produce diminishing returns. At this point
(if it can be detected) the church may harm itself by trying
to grow more. Artificial booster programs such as Sunday
School contests may deceive a church into thinking its optimum point is higher than it really is and cause it to shoot for
an unrealistic goal, suffering frustration when it is not reached.

Perhaps exceptions to this principle can be pointed out, such
as the Little Flock Church in Taipei or the Jotabeche Church
in Santiago; but they do not negate the general principle. If
it is true, then wise churchmen will recognize their point of
optimum growth; and when it is reached, they will think in
terms of starting another church.

4. *Multiplying churches.* The best way for a church to grow
in an urban situation, therefore, is to be active in reproducing
itself. The total number of members of a cathedral church
should not be reckoned in terms of how many are in the immediate congregation only, but that *plus* the members of the
daughter churches. Growth by multiplication is an important
key to urban evangelistic strategy

The famous Brazil for Christ Church in Sao Paulo has discovered this secret. Their big meetings in the cathedral are on
Thursday and Saturday when 5,000 crowd into the partially
constructed building (which eventually will seat 25,000). On
Sunday the attendance drops to something like one hundred
because so many members are in their growing daughter

churches scattered throughout the city, or else they are busy planting new ones.

Julio Castrillo, a successful pastor with the Central American Church in Panama City, says,

> I feel that it is time for a complete revision of our present programs, including the avoidance of the centralization of believers in big churches. . . . We must recognize that multiplication by division is the secret of church growth [1970:9].

Sometimes the possibility of division for growth is threatening, especially when the church loses some old members in order to start a new church elsewhere in the city. The Christian and Missionary Alliance Church in Saigon began to grow like this years ago. Pioneer missionary Irving Stebbins started a new church by removing members from the old one. The church leaders were so disturbed that they went to the national church officers and asked to have the missionary sent home. But on the very Sunday that the new church opened, the Saigon church also had as many in attendance as before; and the Lord has continued to bless both. The mother church now has planted four daughter churches, and the membership in the cathedral church is the same. Its optimum level is about 250, and it has learned the principle of multiplying churches.

If multiplying churches does not become part of the normal activity of city churches, the program of evangelism will probably not be too successful. Wise urban missionary strategy will be built around it.

Six Important Steps for Multiplying Urban Churches

Once we agree with the *principle* of multiplying churches for healthy urban growth, we begin to search for sound *methods*. Unfortunately there is no one recipe that will guarantee success everywhere. But the six steps presented here have proved to be helpful enough in experience so that they can be recommended at least for serious consideration in any urban situation.

1. *Discover the areas of fertile soil.* Well-directed research preliminary to evangelistic efforts takes time, but it will pay

dividends in the long run. The inauguration of the campaign might have to be postponed, but more fruit will be forthcoming. Indiscriminate sowing should be avoided.

One of the receptive areas will usually be the newer working-class neighborhoods. Jesuit Jeffery Klaiber describes the mentality of people who move into these neighborhoods in Lima:

> The typical *barriada* dweller is a man bereft of the ancient values that once sustained him and his family in the rural community where he lived before he migrated to the anonymous and depersonalizing city. He naturally looks forward to a religion in which he can either renew or relive his old values—something that many traditional Catholic churches still offer—or else he looks for a religion that will provide him with a strong sense of belonging or community that he so desperately needs. In many situations, it is the local Evangelical or Adventist church that best fulfills this longing among the uprooted *barriada* dweller [1970:101].

After making a specific study of this matter in Colombia, Edward Murphy has confirmed the fertility of the newer sections. His analysis of a particular campaign states: "The most blessed local church crusades were held in working class *barrio* churches, while the least blessed were held in downtown or upper middle class congregations" (1970:57).

In some areas the high rise apartments are fertile fields, but in others they are barren ground. The thirteen-floor high rise apartments of Singapore are of the fertile variety, according to E. N. Poulson:

> These socially unsettled thousands of people are winnable. . . . Each high rise building has about 1,200 occupants. We believe a church (congregation) can be planted right in the building where the people live. More than a half dozen such churches have emerged as a result of intensive door-to-door evangelism within each building. In some instances services have been held in the flat of a believer. At least three worshipping groups are housed in a groundfloor shop [1970:45].

Whereas the high rises in Singapore apparently are fertile fields, and door-to-door evangelism successfully wins the people, this is not true on the other side of the planet in Buenos Aires, according to Juan Carlos Ortíz. He describes his experience in these words:

> We brought all the believers from outside to visit house-to-house. We visited 10,000 apartments in the high rise buildings, and we did not see any results at all, in spite of a week's work from door-to-door [1969:67].

The places in the city where some churches are already growing give one of the best clues to soil fertility. Some people operate on the mistaken premise that, because a certain neighborhood already has one church, it needs no more. In my opinion, comity agreements in urban situations should be scrapped. If a given church is static, but the neighborhood is receptive, a new dynamic church there may help both of them grow. If the church is already growing, this indicates responsiveness, and new churches are needed since both together will probably not be able to disciple the whole neighborhood. In five years the receptivity may pass, so the harvest should be reaped while it is white.

2. *Set realistic goals.* Without goals, no one can tell where he is heading and how far down the road he might be. If careful research is done ahead of time, it will lead to realistic goal-setting. Long-term goals should provide the framework for short-term goals. The goals should be specific and attainable ones and revised frequently.

Strategy planners recently set a goal of one hundred fifty congregations for Nairobi in 1975, but the goal was criticized by Donald McGavran as inadequate. He says,

> Plans for the cities in Africa must not assume that the slow growth of the past thirty years, heavily subsidized from abroad, will mark the next thirty. *Plans should assume that most of the million can be churched and that this church expansion will pay for itself* [1971:110].

3. *Prepare to sacrifice.* Successful evangelism does not come automatically. It is costly and trying; it requires sacrifices and effort.

It will cost people. Planting new churches will take people from the mother church like the unborn child takes calcium from its mother's bones. But for the joy of the little one, the mother does not complain. A group of people in the mother church who live in the same outlying district can band together to plant a church in that neighborhood. A mother church of three hundred can easily afford fifty people as the seed for a new work or works. The Lord will soon replace the fifty in the mother church, and prepare her for new offspring.

It will cost time. Church-planting evangelism requires time for involvement with the new church members. It may even imply a change in life style, a new circle of friends, and unexpected pastoral obligations. These are very hard adjustments to make, but they are worth it for the extension of the kingdom of God.

It will cost money. The loss of members will mean a loss of income for the mother church. On this basis some pastors discourage church-planting evangelism. The deacons of a church I know well opposed a group of members who wanted to start a new work in their own neighborhood instead of commuting to the downtown cathedral, because they feared a drastic loss of income. But the members persisted, and now the mother church has regained her membership (and her income) while the new church is as large as the mother. Some or all of the budget of many churches, previously invested in active but unfruitful evangelistic efforts, could profitably be channeled to establishing such daughter churches. The mother church could help by buying the lots of new church buildings, as one church in Bogotá, Columbia, does. Soon the new church will be able to support itself, and the funds can be released for other new churches.

It will cost identification. This sacrifice applies most specifically to missionaries. Harry Burke, an urban specialist now in Mexico City, points out that it is very difficult for the ordinary urban missionary to move into the new and receptive areas of the city because of considerations for his family. It seems ironic that the same mentality does not usually exist for identification with a savage jungle tribe. It is necessary to identify, however, if the missionary is going to be fully effective. Burke suggests the creation of a task force of young single people or recently married couples as short-term missionaries to work in urban evangelism. They could properly identify with the people among whom the churches are being planted.

4. *Apply church growth principles.* Some basic principles of church growth are particularly applicable to the urban situation. We will consider several of them at this time.

Prayer. The power of God will not be released except through faithful intercession. The planting of new churches should be an individual and collective prayer burden of the whole congregation. As the congregation unites in prayer, God will move the team out with spiritual power not ctherwise available.

Culture. The people chosen from the mother church to plant a new one should be from approximately the same social and cultural background as those who are to be reached. This should be carefully planned. Don't choose a business executive to evangelize a group of newly-arrived peasants, unless the executive has unusual gifts.

Family units. Concentrate on winning whole families. Don't make the common mistake of starting with children or even with women, at least in patriarchal cultures. If women or children want to become Christians, try to postpone the moment of formal decisions until the father is ready also. If a person truly believes on Christ and has repented of his sin, the formal prayer of decision is probably not the moment of regeneration—God has probably already done a work of grace in the heart. The family is one of the most important keys to growth, and should be handled as a unit like the Philippian jailer and Cornelius. Failure to apply this has brought many evangelistic programs to nought, while the potential for widespread response was there all the time.

The Lutheran World Federation Broadcasting Service in Hong Kong recently conducted a survey to determine the influence leading to faith in students there. One-third of them considered their family as the most important influence, and this factor was at the top of the composite list. The report says:

> In Hong Kong the family is still the basic unit which moulds the child's physical, emotional, mental, and social develop-

ment. The family rated high as the most influential agency in leading the respondents to a religious faith [*The Way*, 1970].

In Japan, the fastest growing church is called Sweet Potato Vine. Their distinctive strategy is based on "cultivating the family stalk." Their efforts always follow family lines, and they feel that this gives much better results than cultivating individual fruit. The church has grown already to be Japan's second largest church (Ray 1971:1).

Homogeneous units. Try not to allow diverse social and cultural elements to mix on the congregation level any more than necessary. Churches must be built as much as possible within homogeneous units if they are to maintain a sense of community among believers. Klaiber sees this operating among Protestants in Peru:

> The congregation is considered not as a congeries of disparate individuals to be "saved" and spiritually cared for, but rather as a tight, well-knit body to be attended to and saved as a community. . . . There is a strong emphasis on such old-fashioned virtues as good-neighborliness, concern and interest in the affairs of others, and open hospitality toward visitors and strangers. Members of the community refer to each other as *hermano* or *hermana*, "brother" or "sister" [1970:101].

5. *Build follow-up into the program.* It has already been mentioned that the problem of effective follow-up is the most needed breakthrough in evangelism in our day. Without pretending to have the answer, I would like to suggest two areas in which better follow-up could be built in from the preliminary planning:

Open-air meetings. The pattern of open-air meetings developed by the Chilean Pentecostal churches has a lesson for all of us. They have avoided turning the meetings into simple "come to our church sometime" services by holding the meetings just prior to their church meetings and inviting the listeners to come right along. Another important feature is that all church members, without exception, are expected to participate in the open-air meetings. This lets the public get a glimpse of a true cross section of the whole church. The open-air meetings end up in the church, not out in the street, this distinguishing them from "multiplying invitations."

Church membership. Commitment to membership in a local church has not been stressed in our traditional urban evangelistic programs. One of Latin America's best-known evangelists once took me out to lunch during a campaign and asked me the reason why more of those who made decisions were not later found in the churches. I reminded him that the night before he had counselled all those who came forward to read their Bibles, pray daily, and tell others about their decision. But he had not counselled them to attend church, much less to be baptized into membership as soon as possible. He accepted the suggestion and began advising them to attend an evangelical church. But the idea that some mechanism be set up in the crusade to encourage them to join churches immediately appeared a bit too radical. It does seem to me, however, that this would be well worth looking into. A decision for Christ in an evangelistic crusade should carry right along with it a firm commitment to become an active member of a local church.

The widespread assumption that interdenominational, city-wide evangelistic efforts make more "impact" has much to commend it. But a question is now being raised in the minds of some churchmen as to whether the interdenominational nature of a crusade might in fact be one of the inhibiting influences on effective follow-up. Some churches which have customarily participated in interdenominational crusades now have decided to concentrate evangelistic efforts on their own local churches, not from a spirit of hostility toward others, but because of a desire for more effectiveness in making disciples.

Juan Carlos Ortíz has developed an unusual evangelistic approach which is giving good results. Evangelism is centered in his local church, the largest Protestant church in Buenos Aires. At the beginning of the sermon, he separates the unbelievers by having them stand, receive the gift of a New Testament, and then go to another room. While Ortíz feeds the Christians, associate evangelists deal with the non-Christians and invite them to accept Christ. Those who do are baptized the same night and become members of the church. Ortíz says,

> When a person is baptized in the name of Jesus Christ there is a higher probability that he will remain faithful. I will give you a statistic: We have calculated that of every hundred people who commit themselves to the Lord and who take the pre-baptismal study course, two or three are baptized, no more. Before they finish the course the rest have disappeared. But if we had baptized the hundred before they had begun the course, twenty would have stayed. How about the eighty? Well, they wouldn't have stayed whether we had baptized them or not [1969:71].

Ortíz' colleague, Keith Bentson, compares the convert to a newborn baby. He asks, "Where do we raise our children? Inside the house or outside? But if we don't baptize new converts, they are outside the house and they know it" (1969: 121).

These ideas might be slightly far out for some of us to accept hastily, and I am not advocating that we do so. But it does appear to be quite certain that a lack of emphasis on the need for baptism and church membership has been a retarding factor in effective follow-up.

6. *Be mobile and flexible.* It is well never to allow a program to become so important that it cannot be changed. Every effort at urban church planting should be to a degree a tentative one. If the effort is unsuccessful, scrap the plan and start again somewhere else. Mobility is one of the great virtues of urban church planting. In Sao Paulo, Donald McGavran set up this rule of thumb for a group laying out a strategy for urban evangelism:

> I counseled them to try neighborhood evangelism for a year, and if at the end of that time they had not assembled a church of at least five *converted* families, to seek a more receptive section of the city. I said "converted families" because it was quite possible to pick up a few second- or third-generation middle class Protestants and form them into a church [1970*b*: 288].

An example of needed flexibility is the difficult university student work in Latin America. Few university student workers are as candid and objective as Jack Voelkel of the Latin America Mission, who has written of the struggle that he and his colleagues are finding in the university community. He mentions that during Evangelism in Depth in Colombia and Peru they "tried everything" with the university students. But in spite of the training manuals, organizational meetings, retreats, and camps "we mobilized almost no Christian students and saw a bare handful of converts" (1969:1). The question to raise concerning this strategic group within the cities is this: Are university students a barren field, or have we been using the wrong methods to reach them?

According to all theories, students should be a fertile field. They are free-thinking enough to look objectively at their traditional religion, they are socially dislocated, they are open to new ideas. Voelkel is seeking the key that will improve the methods of reaching these students in an effective way. But he is flexible enough to recognize that traditional methods have fallen short, and that something different has to be done. This willingness to change is a helpful quality in all urban missionary work.

11

Mission Strategy in Revolutionary Times

ALMOST EVERYBODY wants to get on the revolutionary band-wagon these days. Scarcely a program is proposed without its being billed as "revolutionary" in some sense or other. All this rush toward revolution, however, has diluted the word to the place where hardly anybody knows what it really means. Therefore, prior to discussing what all this has to do with missionary strategy, we must be clear as to what we mean by *revolution.*

We are here thinking of revolution in its socio-political connotation, not in the promotional use of the word which could apply equally to revolutions in Sunday school materials, space travel, soil fertilizers, cake mixes, or even strategy of missions. Furthermore, we do not mean by *revolution* the palace revolts which might change the leaders of a country, but not its social structures. In this sense the word has been used frequently in Latin America where it is said, for example, that "Bolivia has had more revolutions than years of independence." Latin Americanists recognize that since independence Bolivia has had only one real revolution—the social revolution of 1952.

What do we mean, then? Why not let that prolific and persistent defender of revolution, Richard Shaull of Princeton Seminary (whom John Bennett has described as "the chief American theologian concentrating on these issues"), define it for us:

> In a revolutionary situation the political task is primary, but that task is defined in a special way. It is a question of power to overcome the old order and create a new order; for that reason the goal can never be the mere conquest of power within the old structures. Only the destruction of the old structure of power and its replacement by a new constitutes a revolution [1970:35].

198

Whereas I expressed my thorough disagreement with Shaull's theological position in an earlier book, I must accept his definition of revolution as what informed people in the Third World mean when they use the term. Its Marxist overtones are evident; and Shaull's own precarious theological position is exposed when, after giving the above definition, he makes the statement, "As Marx clearly understood, this is ultimately the question of the creation of a new man"(Ibid.).

While evangelicals reject the theology that is now being called "revolutionary humanism" (Raines and Dean 1970), they do not reject the concerns for social justice, world peace, opportunities for economic equality, and other expressions of loving one's neighbor which unfortunately are often articulated much more eloquently by the radical left than by Bible-believing Christians. Many present members of the evangelical university student generation are disturbed by the fact that Herbert Marcuse turns them on more than Billy Graham, but at the same time they are honest enough to admit it and seek biblical answers to their dilemma. It is not easy to distinguish clearly between the motives behind revolution and the methods and ideologies applied to implement them; but if we attempt to do this, we will help ourselves as missionaries in revolutionary times.

THE MISSIONARY'S ATTITUDE TOWARD REVOLUTION

Perhaps the revolutionary spirit is stronger in Latin America than in other parts of the Third World at this time. Reports from the Geneva Conference on Church and Society in 1966 indicate that "usually strong and radical voices from Latin America kept this form of revolution before the conference" (Bennett 1970:64). For this reason the opinion of one of Latin America's notable evangelical leaders, Rubén Lores, needs to be heard. Lores says,

> Strangely enough, the majority of missionaries who come here from the United States are not well equipped to work in this revolutionary atmosphere. . . . Their country had its revolution—calmer and better-reasoned—generations ago. They are

the heirs of that revolution, and they themselves don't know how to act in a revolution [1964:1].

The cultural overhang that Lores puts his finger on can hinder the effectiveness of northern missionaries ministering in the Third World today. I see two particularly dangerous expressions of this weakness. The first is a *blanket opposition to revolution*. Many Americans reject revolution categorically as a political option. This is perfectly understandable for a middle-class adult resident of the United States, as Lores hints. The average American would be ridiculous to want to change a social structure which so evidently favors him. Carl Henry, as one of the principal theological spokesmen of this segment of society says:

> While under some conditions Christian conscience may indeed approve certain *consequences* of revolution, Christian social theory neither promotes nor approves revolution itself as a method of social transformation [1964:176].

In the northern countries, most evangelicals would agree with Henry, although students, hippies, blacks, and Chicanos might not. But very few evangelical thinkers in the Third World, especially in Latin America would agree. Many, while critical of Marxist atheism, materialism, the dialectical interpretation of history, and naturalistic anthropology, nevertheless see little inherent disharmony between Marxist political, social, and economic ideology and Christianity. On one occasion I raised the following question in a Bolivian seminary class: "Can a Christian be a Marxist?" The immediate reply, predictably, was, "Can he be anything else?"

Northern evangelicals might wish this were not the case in Latin America and other parts of the Third World, but wishes will not change the situation. Revolution is a fact of life there, and a factor to which sound missionary strategy will have to adapt.

The second aspect of cultural overhang that can hinder missionary work is the other extreme: *the urge for the participation of churches in political revolution*. Some missionaries come from large denominations which in their homelands exert considerable political influence. They think it is normal for churches to make political pronouncements and enter into political activities. This is not valid for the small churches and denominations found in the Third World. As McGavran says:

> In a land where the Church is a tiny minority—and this is the case in most lands of Africasia—large social action can scarcely be expected. It is sheer nonsense to expect a tiny Church to "thunder" against social injustice [1965:49].

Realism must temper the Christian attitude toward social changes when Third World churches are involved. This is not to say that the Christian community should be silent, especially on clearly moral (as contrasted to purely political) issues. In Japan legalized prostitution was recently rescinded, and the organized effort of Christians in Japan was an important factor in bringing about new laws (Gingerich 1968:175). Some will say that political action was involved when the law was changed, and this is true. But it was over an issue upon which the church could take a united stand. The churches I know do not usually enjoy equal unity when it comes to choosing political options, and efforts toward unified action can easily cause bitterness and splits in the body of Christ, as many churches in Cuba have learned. Individual Christians should be active in political parties, and the church should encourage them, but under no circumstances should the church, as church, take political sides.

A STAND FOR SOCIAL JUSTICE

One of the moral issues upon which Christians, including missionaries, should take a clear stand is that of social justice. The Scriptures are emphatic that God stands with the poor when they clamor for equal social, political and economic opportunities. The Epistle of James, for example, powerfully indicates that God dislikes the oppression of the poor by the privileged rich. Where existing social structures perpetuate oppression, the Christian conscience should demand a change in those structures. This does not mean that a missionary should take political sides in the host country, or that he should actively promote any one interpretation of how the oppressive social structures can best be altered. But as to God's will for social justice he should not be silent, because silence itself can easily be interpreted as a stance for the status quo. As Jaymes Morgan once said:

> The politics of silence—the art of doing and saying nothing —is in actuality forceful social action in behalf of the status quo. It is as assuredly social action as any of the more easily recognized varieties, such as sit-ins and freedom marches. . . . You and I mount the podium of our moral dignity and shout for all the world to hear that the guilt of World War II and the race-murder of six million lies not alone at the door of war criminals, but at the door of the German people. Why? Most of them did nothing. Which is precisely the point [1967:2].

Missionaries, in teaching the whole counsel of God, must not neglect to communicate their feelings in favor of social reform where it is needed. In a revolutionary situation a missionary who is labeled as a reactionary or a counterrevolutionary may lose much effectiveness, and this is especially valid when he is a North American. While it is true that a minority may not be able to do much, as Horace Fenton says, "the fact that we cannot do everything is no reason for not doing anything" (1969:5). Missionaries should teach principles of social justice, then give liberty to believers to participate in any political movement that they themselves may judge as the best means to accomplish those ends in their particular country. If they choose a revolutionary method as over against a "developmentist" position (which would more clearly represent United States foreign policy), they should feel at liberty to do so.

How Revolution May Help the Church

In some ways revolution may help church growth. Those interested in planning effective strategy will be interested in observing revolutions in any part of the world and their effects on people. In many cases revolution will cause people who were formerly oppressed to be receptive to the gospel. Christ as Liberator has a strong appeal. A complete break with the past implies for many people a break also from their nonchristian religion, the religion associated with the oppressors.

Revolution often frees previously enslaved minds. Oppressed peoples have little freedom of choice, or little incentive toward creativity. They do and think what they are told. If revolution accomplishes its goal of humanizing men and women, it will free them to make choices, and open them for new ideas. Perhaps for the first time they will dare to give serious consideration to the gospel message. New wineskins are ready for new wine.

Finally, revolution may free a people to develop a more culturally-relevant expression of their Christianity. Self-determination will help them shed western trappings, think independently, and emerge with a particular expression of Christianity which makes more sense to the people in general than it ever has before. This is especially true when the revolution carries with it the rejection of strong colonialist or imperialist influences.

HOW THE CHURCH MAY HELP REVOLUTION

If we continue to grant that the objectives of revolution (utopian as they may be) are good for people, the church will want to contribute wherever possible. By providing regenerated leaders with the moral fiber to give the revolution permanency and help keep it from corruption, the church can make its most important contribution. Ralph Winter compares these people to building materials:

> The most radical revolution in history has been the revolution in the lives of the believers. . . . This is like the appearance of a new and high quality building material. It is in itself the basic revolution. . . . With this new material, governments of a new and different and superior type can be built. No truly modern government can succeed without a certain minimum percentage of men of high integrity [1967:223].

In many places the very transformation of men by the power of the Holy Spirit has provided materials for a new social construction. Paul Enyart tells of the experience of Asapalpa, Honduras, which was a town notorious throughout the whole region for terror and crime, drunkenness and brawling, hatred and murder. Ordinary people dared not go out in the streets after dark for fear of their lives. Then one day the village chief opened his heart to the gospel. His life and scores of others were transformed by the power of the Spirit of God. Now a large, new church has been built. The odd people in town are those who are *not* Christians. Peace and contentment reigns. The crime rate has dropped to practically zero, and villagers stroll the streets at night in perfect safety. The goals of the most idealistic revolutionary have actually been fulfilled in Asapalpa, all through the work of Christ Himself.

The church can help the revolution not only by providing the human building materials that will make the best possible kind of society, but also by speaking to the moral implications of social issues with a prophetic voice. The Word of God touches the heart of every plank in the revolutionary platform which will benefit the human race. The church can not only preach on love and justice, but it can proclaim the means by which the new man whose life will be characterized by these virtues may be created. In this respect, the church (or more accurately, the Holy Spirit) can do what revolution cannot do. As René Padilla says,

> Revolution does not change man; it does not touch the root of social evils. For this reason, as soon as the revolutionary regime is established the injustices of the old order reappear and the revolutionary class becomes a new oligarchy [1969: 19].

McGavran points out that "When ordinary men come to power, they feather their own nests. It takes extraordinary men, men in Christ, to come to power and triumph over the temptations of selfishness" (1965*b*:50).

DANGERS INHERENT IN REVOLUTION

The Christian view of revolution must be a critical one. Whereas a prophetic Christian voice is expected to denounce social injustices, the same voice is expected to denounce the revolution when it goes astray.

The revolution, for example, may turn demonic. It may become totalitarian, absolutist, and idolatrous. It may become antichristian, taking legal measures to stamp out the Christian church as it has done in Mainland China and North Korea, where the church was considered to a degree a western cultural incursion.

At times the revolution may maintain a facade of religious freedom, but restrict freedom of activity so as to hinder or prevent healthy church growth. The state may promote a materialistic philosophy, or make laws which subject the church to the state. If the church is considered to be the opiate of the people, this type of repression is to be anticipated and avoided where possible.

Within the context of the church, the revolution may fascinate some Christians so much that it eventually corrupts their theology. Some revolutionary-minded theologians have come up with dangerous syncretisms between Marxist ideology and Christian theology. In a criticism of the 1966 Geneva Conference on Church and Society, René Padilla has said concerning the "theology of revolution":

> Instead of showing the relevance of Revelation to Revolution, it makes Revolution the source of Revelation . . . The "theology of revolution" is in essence a new version of the "other gospel" that Paul combatted so vigorously in the first century [1969:20].

In this perspective, working for the revolution or "helping God work out His purposes in history" becomes the chief end of Christian mission. But it is sub-Christian when the church deceives itself into thinking that it is really the opiate of the people, and wishes itself out of existence so the revolution can move forward. Christians who seek the demise of the church have misinterpreted and misused the revolution, allowing it to corrupt them.

Revolutionary zeal may create another false impression. It may lead some to believe the myth that where social justice and economic equality prevail, people will be more receptive to the gospel. Therefore, some Christians, such as Camilo Torres, declare themselves for revolution first, until the cause of justice wins out. Then, they say, they will return to the church. McGavran has exposed this fallacy, however, as follows:

> It is theoretically possible that if the Church were to manifest

great concern for social justice and were to redeem some section of society from its bonds, notable growth of the Church would follow. This, however, is not what one usually finds. The social reformation in England did not give rise to the Baptist and Methodist churches. It was the other way around [1965*a*:2].

Another danger of revolution is that the enthusiasm it generates may produce a false dichotomy between social action and church planting. Some think a moratorium has to be called on evangelism in order to get on properly with the revolution. Many who have given body and soul to the revolution have no time for soul-winning. They turn from church planting to serving good social causes. Harold Lindsell sees this danger specifically among evangelicals. He warns,

> I predict evangelicals will become substantially involved in socio-political affairs at the expense of proclamation. . . . It seems particularly difficult for groups to keep a respectable balance between proclamation and service and wherever the emphasis has swung to service it has always come at the expense of proclamation. I foresee that this same trend will occur among evangelicals [1969:9].

The final danger, and perhaps the most deadly, is that the revolution, if misdirected, may split the body of Christ. Some Christians may become so deeply involved in one political stance that they are intolerant of other options, even among brethren in Christ. They cannot bring themselves to permit liberty among Christians in the political sphere, and thus they become the cause of divisions in the church. It is God's will that peace and mutual love prevail among Christian people. Only a corrupt revolution or a corrupted revolutionary will allow this peace to be broken for political reasons.

MISSIONARY STRATEGY IN REVOLUTION

In conclusion, several principles should be kept in mind when missionary strategy is being planned for a revolutionary situation, whether it be an entire country such as Chile or a subculture such as the United States blacks.

1. Do not allow the church to project a counterrevolution-

ary image. Where revolution is seen by the majority as the best way toward social justice, the church should not be thought of as a negative influence. Most revolutionaries, from reading Marx and Mao, have built-in prejudices against the church as it is, and the church itself need not provide more fuel for the fire.

2. At the same time, do not allow the church as an institution to become identified with any particular political expression. While speaking with a clear voice on social issues, the church should maintain political transcendence.

3. Seek out peoples whose way of life is being changed by the revolution, win them to Christ, and vigorously plant churches among them.

4. Engage, as a church, in meaningful and tangible programs of social service. The public should know that the church is concerned for the poor and dispossessed. As Horace Fenton says:

> In carrying out a ministry of compassion in a revolution-scarred land, we must engage in (and encourage the churches to engage in) activities that will feed the hungry, clothe the naked, and provide for the fatherless [1969:5].

5. Finally, do not confuse the priorities of God's commands to the church. History has shown how easy it is for the Christian church to become so enthusiastic about meeting social needs that the spiritual needs of men take a back seat or in some cases are forgotten. God's Word is clear as to priorities for the church. While we should reject the dichotomy that unnaturally divides man's body from his soul, we do not let ourselves be deafened to Christ's words, "Fear not them [both indviduals and social structures?] who kill the body, but are not able to kill the soul; but rather fear him who is able to destroy both *soul* and *body* in hell" (Mt 10:28). Christ gives clear priority to the eternal destiny of the whole man over his temporal condition when the choice must be made.

Specifically in the context of revolution, Vernon Grounds has expressed this very well:

> What is the Church's distinctive task, anyway? Is it to spearhead revolution? Of course not! Is it, on the contrary, to protect the American way of life? To defend free enterprise?

To save Western civilization with all those institutions and ideals that have been inspired and sired by the Bible? Again, of course not! . . . The Church's task is evangelism and witness and mission, worship and education and fellowship [1971:5].

In *The Social Conscience of the Evangelical,* Sherwood Wirt, with his inimitable style, describes this matter of priorities and the danger the church runs by confusing them. His statement furnishes a fitting conclusion to this chapter, and the book:

> When social action is mistaken for evangelism the church has ceased to manufacture its own blood cells and is dying of leukemia. When social action becomes more important than evangelism the church has forgotten to breathe and is already dead of heart failure [1968:129].

My prayer, and yours, I am sure, is for a healthy, red-blooded church, fearlessly moving into the world under the power of the Holy Spirit, to proclaim good tidings to the meek, to bind up the broken-hearted, to proclaim liberty to the captives and declare the acceptable year of the Lord; making disciples, planting churches, and rejoicing at the growth and glory of the kingdom of God before Christ comes once again to take us to Himself.

Bibliography

ALLEN, Roland
1962 *Missionary Methods: St. Paul's or Ours?* Grand Rapids: Eerdmans.
ALLIANCE WITNESS
1970 "Presstime Paragraphs for Your Information and Intercession." May 27.
BAAGO, Kaj
1966 "The Post-Colonial Crisis of Missions." *International Review of Missions* 55 (No. 219, July): 322-332. (Geneva)
BANKS, Donald
1968 "In Africa Evangelism Is 'In'," *World Vision Magazine*, December, pp. 17-19.
BARKMAN, Paul F.; DAYTON, Edward R.; and GRUMAN, Edward L.
1969 *Christian Collegians and Foreign Missions*. Monrovia: Missions Advanced Research and Communications Center.
BARRETT, David B.
1968 *Schism and Renewal in Africa, An Analysis of Six Thousand Contemporary Religious Movements*. Nairobi: Oxford University Press.
BARRIENTOS, Alberto
1970 "El Uso del Templo." ¡En Marcha! Internacional 17 (julio-diciembre): 6-8. (San José de Costa Rica)
1971 *Paraguay para Cristo, Instrucción básica de Evangelismo a Fondo*. Asunción, Paraguay: Evangelismo a Fondo.
BAVINCK, J. H.
1964 *An Introduction to the Science of Missions*. Philadelphia: Presbyterian and Reformed Publishing Company.
BENNETT, John C.
1970 "Christian Responsibility in a Time That Calls for Revolutionary Change." In *Marxism and Radical Religion*, ed. John C. Raines and Thomas Dean. Philadelphia: Temple University Press.
BENTSON, Keith
1969 See ORTIZ, Juan Carlos and BENTSON, Keith.
BEYERHAUS, Peter
1971 *Missions: Which Way? Humanization or Redemption*. Grand Rapids: Eerdmans.

209

BEYERHAUS, Peter, and LEFEVER, Henry
1964 *The Responsibile Church and the Foreign Missions.* Grand
    Rapids: Eerdmans.
BLACK, David R.
1970 *Letter to Evangelical Missions Quarterly* 9 (No. 3,
    Spring): 191-192.
BOWERS, W. Paul
1965 "Why Are Evangelicals Overlooking Mission Theology?"
    Christianity Today, September 10, pp. 5-7.
BRADSHAW, Malcolm R.
1969 *Church Growth through Evangelism in Depth.* South
    Pasadena: William Carey Library.
CASTRILLO, Julio
1970 "Let's Turn the World Upside Down." *Central American
    Bulletin,* January-February, pp. 8-9.
CHRISTIANITY TODAY
1969 "Mission and Missionaries: 1969." April 25, pp. 20-21.
CHUA Wee Hian
1969 "Encouraging Missionary Movement in Asian Churches."
    Christianity Today 3 (No. 19, June 20): 9-12.
COLEMAN, Robert E.
1964 *The Master Plan of Evangelism.* Old Tappan: Revell.
COX, Harvey
1966 "Mission in a World of Cities." *International Review of
    Missions* 55 (No. 219, July): 273-281. (Geneva)
DAVIS, Raymond J.
1970 "Survival in the 70's." *International Christian Broad-
    casters Bulletin,* September, pp. 3ff.
DAYTON, Edward R.
1968 "Does Technology Exclude the Holy Spirit?" *World Vision
    Magazine* 12 (No. 9, October): 6.
1971 "Information—Who Needs it?" *MARC News-letter,* Janu-
    ary, pp. 1-2.
DOUGLAS, J. D.
1962 "Disciple." In *The New Bible Dictionary,* ed. J. D. Doug-
    glas. Grand Rapids: Eerdmans.
ECUMENICAL REVIEW
1971 "Common Witness and Proselytism, A Study Document."
    Vol. 23 (No. 1, January): 9-20. (Geneva, World Coun-
    cil of Churches)
ELLIOT, Elizabeth
1968 *Who Shall Ascend, the Life of R. Kenneth Strachan of
    Costa Rica,* New York: Harper & Row.

ENNS, Arno W.
1971 *Man, Milieu and Mission in Argentina.* Grand Rapids: Eerdmans.

ENYART, Paul
1970*a* "Sinful to Number?" *Church Growth Bulletin* 6 (No. 3, January): 43.
1970*b* *Friends in Central America.* South Pasadena: William Carey Library.

FENTON, Horace L.
1965 "The Demands of the Impossible." *World Vision Magazine,* May, pp. 11, 30.
1969 "Missions and Revolution." *Latin America Evangelist,* March-April, pp. 3-5. (Bogota)
1970 "Evangelism in Depth." In *Mobilizing for Saturation Evangelism,* ed. Clyde W. Taylor and Wade T. Coggins. Wheaton, Ill.: Evangelical Missions Information Service.

FISKE, Edward B.
1966 "The Social Activists and the Evangelists." *New York Times,* December 10.

FLATT, Donald C.
1970 "In search of God's Bridge for Mission: a Critique of the Church Growth Philosophy." *World Vision Magazine,* January, pp. 18-20.

FORSBERG, Malcolm I.
1968 "The Missionary Should 'Advertise' the Encouraging Side of His Story." *Christian Times* 2 (No. 11, March 17): 2.

FULTON, C. Darby
1968 "Mission-Church Relations: Integrate or Cooperate?" *Evangelical Missions Quarterly* 4 (No. 2, Winter): 65-74.

GELDENHUYS, Norval
1950 *Commentary on the Gospel of Luke.* London: Marshall, Morgan, & Scott.

GINGRICH, Melvin
1968 *The Christian and Revolution.* Scottsdale: Herald Press.

GLASSER, Arthur F.
1969 "What Has Been the Evangelical Stance, New Delhi to Uppsala?" *Evangelical Missions Quarterly* 5 (No. 3, Spring): 129-150.
1971*a* "Theology: With or Without the Bible." *Church Growth Bulletin* 7 (No. 3, January): 112-114.
1971*b* "Straws in the Wind." *Church Growth Bulletin* 7 (No. 3, January): 117-119.

1971c "Thinking about Jerico in Ethiopia—What Would You Do?" *Church Growth Bulletin* 7 (No. 3, January): 116-117.

GONZALEZ, Justo L.
1969 *The Development of Christianity in the Latin Caribbean.* Grand Rapids: Eerdmans.

GREEN, Michael
1970 *Evangelism in the Early Church.* Grand Rapids: Eerdmans.

GROUNDS, Vernon C.
1971 "Bombs or Bibles? Get Ready for Revolution!" *Christianity Today* 15 (No. 8, January 15): 4-6.

HAY, Alexander Rattray
1947 *The New Testament Order for Church and Missionary.* 2 ed. Temperley: New Testament Missionary Union.

HAY, Ian M.
1972 "The Emergence of a Missionary-Minded Church in Nigeria." In *Church/Mission Tensions Today,* ed. C. Peter Wagner. Chicago: Moody Press.

HENRY, Carl F. H.
1964 *Aspects of Christian Social Ethics.* Grand Rapids: Eerdmans.

HENRY, Carl F. H. and MOONEYHAM, W. Stanley, eds.
1967 *One Race, One Gospel, One Task, World Congress on Evangelism, Berlin 1966, Official Reference Volumes.* Vols. 1 and 2. Minneapolis: World Wide Publications.

HILLIS, Dick
n.d. *I Was Never Called.* Overseas Crusades. (Pamphlet)

HILLIS, Don
1968 "I Was a Flagellant." *The Presbyterian Journal,* October 23, p. 9.

HORNER, Norman A., ed.
1968 *Protestant Crosscurrents in Mission, the Ecumenical-Conservative Encounter.* Nashville: Abingdon.

HOWARD, David M.
1970a *Student Power in World Evangelism.* Downer's Grove: Inter-Varsity Press.
1970b *Don't Wait for the Macedonians.* Wheaton: Evangelical Missions Information Service. (Pamphlet)

IRWIN, Franklin
n.d. "Evangelism Deep and Wide." Christian & Missionary Alliance. (Mimeographed paper circulated in Viet Nam)

KENNY, Joseph
1970 "Reassessment of Apostolate Among Muslims." *Inter-*

national Review of Mission 59 (No. 233, January): 32-38. (Geneva)

KING, Louis
n.d. Mimeographed paper.

KITTLE, Gerhard
1967 *Theological Dictionary of The New Testament.* Vol. 4. Grand Rapids: Eerdmans.

KLAIBER, Jeffery
1970 "Pentacostal Breakthrough." *America* 122 (January 31): 99-102.

KRAFT, Charles H.
1971 "The New Wine of Independence." *World Vision Magazine,* February, pp. 6-9.

KRASS, Alfred C.
1971 "Evangelism—Understanding Our Presuppositions." In *The Whole Earth Newsletter.* New York: United Church of Christ.

LAGEER, Eileen
1970 *New Life for All, True Accounts of In-Depth Evangelism in West Africa.* Chicago: Moody.

LALIVE d'EPINAY, Christian
1969 *Haven of the Masses: A Study of the Pentecostal Movement in Chile.* New York: Friendship Press.

LATIN AMERICA MISSION
n.d. *New Dimension in Evangelism.* Bogota, N.J. (Booklet)
1971 "Prayer and Visitation Bring Results in Mexico's Evangelism in Depth." Mexico City: Latin America Mission. (News release)

LATIN AMERICA PULSE
1970 "Summary Report/Consultation on Latin America." Wheaton: Evangelical Committee on Latin America.

LEFEVER, Henry
1964 See BEYERHAUS, Peter and LEFEVER, Henry. (Lefever writes the Introduction to Beyerhaus' book.)

LINDSELL, Harold
1969 "As I See the Future." *The Presbyterian Journal,* July 23, pp. 9-11.

LORES, Rubén
1964 "Today's Battle—Today's Weapons." *Latin America Evangelist,* January-February, p. 1. (Bogota)
1967 "Evangelism in Depth." In *One Race, One Gospel, One Task,* ed. Carl F. H. Henry and Stanley Mooneyham. Vol. 2. Minneapolis: World Wide Publishers.

1970 "Mobilization of Believers and Churches for Evangelism."
In *Mobilizing for Saturation Evangelism,* ed. Clyde W.
Taylor and Wade Coggins. Wheaton: Evangelical Missions Information Service.

MC GAVRAN, Donald A.
1965*a* "Social Justice and Evangelism." *World Vision Magazine,* June.
1965*b* "What Meaning Does the Revolution Have for the Christian Mission?" *Church Growth Bulletin* 6 (1969: 47-51.
1969 "Radio and Church Growth." *Church Growth Bulletin* 6 (No. 2, November): 17.
1970*a* "For Such a Time as This." Unpublished address delivered at School of Missions publicity banquet, Pasadena, February.
1970*b* *Understanding Church Growth.* Grand Rapids: Eerdmans.
1970*c* "The Right and Wrong of the Presence Idea of Mission." *Evangelical Missions Quarterly* 6 (No. 2, Winter): 98-109.
1971 "Urban Church Planting." *Church Growth Bulletin* 8 (1971): 110.

MACKAY, John A.
1969 *Christian Reality and Appearance.* Richmond: John Knox.

MAHER, Charles
1968 "Off the Field, Players Do Not Mix So Well." *Los Angeles Times,* March 29, Section III, pp. 1ff.

MANGHAM, Jr., T. Grady
1972 "Developing Church Responsibility in Viet Nam." In *Church/Mission Tensions Today,* ed. C. Peter Wagner. Chicago: Moody Press.

MICHENER, James A.
1969 "Those Fabulous Italian Designers." *Reader's Digest,* September, pp. 157-66.

MISSIONS ADVANCED RESEARCH -AND COMMUNICATION CENTER
1971 *Continuing Evangelism in Brazil.* Monrovia: MARC.

MOFFETT, Samuel
1969 "What is Evangelism?" *Christianity Today* 13 (No. 24, September 12): 13-14.

MOONEYHAM, W. Stanley
1970 "Evangelism: The Church Has Played It Safe Too Long." *World Vision Magazine* 14 (No. 8, September).

MORGAN, Jaymes P., Jr.
1967 "An Evangelical Looks at Social Concern in Light of the Racial Problem." Unpublished address given at National Association of Evangelicals luncheon, Los Angeles, April 5.
MURPHY, Edward F.
1970 "Follow Through Evangelism in Latin America." In *Mobilizing for Saturation Evangelism,* ed. Clyde W. Taylor and Wade T. Coggins. Wheaton Ill.: Evangelical Missions Information Service.
NEILL, Stephen
1967 *The Unfinished Task.* London: Edinburgh House Press.
NEWBIGIN, Lesslie
1960 "Mission and Missions." *Christianity Today,* August 1, p. 23. (Spoken to the 172nd General Assembly of the United Presbyterian Church in the U.S.A.)
ORCHARD, R. K.
1964 *Missions in a Time of Testing, Thought and Practice in Contemporary Missions.* London: Lutterworth Press.
ORITZ, Juan Carlos and BENTSON, Keith
1969 *. . . y será predicado este evangelio.* Buenos Aires: Logos.
PACKER, J. I.
1961 *Evangelism and the Sovereignty of God.* Downer's Grove: Inter-Varsity Press.
PADILLA, C. René
1969 "Revolution and Revelation." *Themelios* 6 (No. 3/4, Winter): pp. 15-23. (Lausanne, IFES)
1971 "A Steep Climb Ahead for Theology in Latin America." *Evangelical Missions Quarterly* 7 (No. 2, Winter): 99-106.
PARKER, Pierson
1962 "Disciple." In *The Interpreter's Dictionary of The Bible,* Vol. 1. New York: Abingdon.
PETERS, George W.
1970a *Saturation Evangelism.* Grand Rapids: Zondervan.
1970b "An Analysis from Africa." *Africa Pulse* 1 (No. 2, March).
1971 "The Missionary of the Seventies." *Bibliotheca Sacra* 128 (No. 509, January-March): 50-61.
PLUMMER, Alfred
1901 *A Critical and Exegetical Commentary on the Gospel According to S. Luke.* Edinburgh: T. & T. Clark.

POULSON, E. N.
  1970 "Every Thirteen Story Building a Parish." *Church Growth Bulletin* 6 (No. 3): 45-46.
RAINES, John C., and DEAN, Thomas, eds.
  1970 *Marxism and Radical Religion, Essays Toward a Revolutionary Humanism.* Philadelphia: Temple University Press.
RAY, Chandu
  1971a *COAFE Newsletter,* January. (Singapore, Coordinating Office for Asian Evangelism)
  1971b *COAFE Newsletter,* March.
  1971c *COAFE Newsletter,* May.
READ, William; MONTERROSO, Victor M.; and JOHNSON, Harmon A.
  1969 *Latin American Church Growth.* Grand Rapids: Eerdmans.
REES, Paul S.
  1968a "The Myth of Ecumenism." *World Vision Magazine* 12 (No. 6, July-August): 47.
  1968b " 'Called' or not 'Called'?" *World Vision Magazine,* May, p. 48.
  1969 "The Myth of Parallelism." *World Vision Magazine* 13 (No. 3, March): 48.
  1971 "I Have My Doubts," *World Vision Magazine,* January, p. 32.
ROBERTS, W. Dayton
  1967 *Revolution in Evangelism: The Story of Evangelism in Depth in Latin America.* Chicago: Moody.
ROWEN, Samuel F.
  1971 "Should We Drop the Term 'Missionary'?" *Evangelical Missions Quarterly* 7 (No. 2, Winter): 92-98.
SANDERS, Robert
  1969 "Mission Launch on the Amazon." *The Life of Faith,* October 11, pp. 9-10. (London)
SCHERER, James A.
  1964 *Missionary, Go Home!* Englewood Cliffs: Prentice-Hall.
SHAULL, Richard
  1970 "The End of the Road and a New Beginning." In *Marxism and Radical Religion,* eds. John C. Raines and Thomas Dean. Philadelphia: Temple University Press.
STRACHAN, R. Kenneth
  1964 "Call to Witness." *International Review of Missions* 53

(No. 210, April): 191-200. (Geneva, World Council of Churches)

1968 *The Inescapable Calling.* Grand Rapids: Eerdmans.

TAHMAZIAN, Dionisio

1969 "¿Qué papel cumplen las agencias misioneras?" *Destellos Evangélicos,* No. 152 (septiembre). (Montevideo)

TIME MAGAZINE

1968 "The Faith of Soul and Slavery." April 19, p. 70.

TIPPETT, A. R.

1969 *Verdict Theology in Missionary Theory.* Lincoln, Ill.: Lincoln Christian College Press.

U.S. NEWS & WORLD REPORT

1968 "Where the Churches are in Trouble." February 26, pp. 74-76.

1970 "Big Gains for Christian Faiths in Black Africa," December 28, pp. 50-52.

VANDEVORT, Eleanor C.

1969 "Does the Great Commission Require Great Success?" *Eternity,* March, pp. 28-29.

VISCHER, Lukas

1969 "Report of Joint Working Group between Roman Catholic Church and the World Council of Churches to the WCC Central Committee, August, 1969 (Canterbury)." *The Ecumenical Review,* October, p. 358. (Geneva)

VOELKEL, Jack

1969 "Our Struggle in the Latin Universities." *Latin America Evangelist,* September-October, pp. 1-4. (Bogota)

WAGNER, C. Peter

1970 *The Protestant Movement in Bolivia.* South Pasadena: William Carey Library.

WARD, Ted

1971 *Memo for the Underground.* Carol Stream, Ill.: Creation House.

WARREN, Max, ed.

1971 *To Apply the Gospel, Selections from Writings of Henry Venn.* Grand Rapids: Eerdmans.

WAY, THE

1970 "Hong Kong Youth Confronts Religion." *The Way,* No. 3, pp. 22-28. (Singapore, IFES)

WEBSTER, Warren

1971 "The Coming Breakthrough in Asia." *His Magazine,* January, pp. 14-16.

WELD, Wayne C.
  1968 *An Ecuadorian Impasse.* Chicago: Dept. of World Mis-
         sions, Evangelical Covenant Church of America.
  1969 *Principios del Crecimiento de la Iglesia.* Mimeographed
         edition. Medellín: Seminario Bíblico Unido.
WESCOTT, B. F.
  1951 *The Gospel According to St. John.* Grand Rapids: Eerd-
         mans.
WHITE, John
  1967 "Missions and Proselytism." *His Magazine,* November,
         pp. 10-14.
WILLEMS, Emilio
  1967 *Followers of the New Faith: Culture Change and the Rise
         of Protestantism in Brazil and Chile.* Nashville: Vander-
         bilt University Press.
WILLIAMS, Colin
  1966 *Faith in a Secular Age.* New York: Harper & Row.
WILLOUGHBY, William
  1969 "Storefront   Churches: Social   Stabilizers." *Christianity
         Today,* May 9, pp. 44-45.
WINTER, Ralph D.
  1967 "Revolution,   Communism,   Democracy   and   Church
         Growth." *Church Growth Bulletin* 6:222-223.
  1970 Letter to *Evangelical Missions Quarterly* 7 (No. 1, Fall):
         55.
  1971a "The New Missions and the Mission of the Church." *The
         International Review of Missions* 60 (No. 237, January):
         89-100. (Geneva)
  1971b *The Warp and The Woof, Organizing for Mission.* South
         Pasadena: William Carey Library. (R. Pierce Beaver
         writes one chapter in the book.)
  1972 "Planting Younger Missions," in *Church/Mission Ten-
         sions Today,* ed. C. Peter Wagner. Chicago: Moody Press.
WIRT, Sherwood Eliot
  1968 *The Social Conscience of the Evangelical.* New York:
         Harper & Row.
WONDERLY, William L.
  1966 "At Home in a Second Language." *Practical Anthropol-
         ogy,* May-June, pp. 97-102.
WORLD STUDENT CHRISTIAN FEDERATION
  1965 *Student World* 58 (No. 3). (Geneva)
YUEN, Peter
  1970 "The Acts of the Asians." *The Way,* No. 2, pp. 7-11.
         (Singapore, IFES)

Subject Index

Scripture Index